40 DAYS TO FREEDOM
A GUIDE TO RELEASING THE PAST TO EMBRACE YOUR FUTURE

For more books and products, visit:
www.charityisrael.net

DREAMSTART PUBLISHING

TABLE OF CONTENTS

Dear Reader,

Thanks so much for investing in my dream of becoming an author. Writing a book is one thing, but someone purchasing it is a miracle! I truly appreciate it, and I pray your life is challenged and changed as mine was writing it. I can guarantee you that this book will make you uncomfortable as some of the truths of my life are not beautiful. I pray instead of passing judgement, you would allow the truths of your life to be unveiled. I am certain you will laugh at a few of my foolish decisions, and you will be in awe of the amazing love of God. In this book you will find:

- Freedom Questions: Questions created to help you discover and speak some truths about your own life.

- Freedom Assignments: These are a few of the things I did to break bad habits, cultivate discipline in my life, and change my stinking thinking.

- Freedom Prayers: These are honest prayers I have prayed to God concerning the areas in my life that his love, forgiveness, and grace were desperately needed.

My prayer for you as you read this book is that the love, grace, forgiveness, and truth of who God is would overtake your soul. As you see parts of yourself through my experiences, may FREEDOM come to your soul; and make its residence in your heart. Lastly, may you find joy in being "a new creation" in Christ.

Excited about Your Future,
Charity Israel

Dear Child,

"Build me an altar with your life as the sacrifice. Surrender everything! Place all of who you are on it that I may consume every part of you that is not of Me. Stay still for the purification and allow my Word to cleanse you. You have given your time and energy to everyone else. Now it is time to give your time and energy to knowing who you are in me. Your freedom is contingent upon receiving forgiveness of your Past. Acceptance of who you will only happen when you realize who you are in Me. You will never live in love until you entrust me with your fears, failures, and pain. I long to heal you, but you must first lay yourself on the altar (in my presence). It is where the desires of your spirit will be manifested, and others will come to see you have changed through me."

With Love,
Your Heavenly Father

DAY 1
God Did You Really Mean Marvelous?

You made all the delicate, inner parts of my body and knit me together in my mother's womb. 14 Thank you for making me so wonderfully complex. Your workmanship is marvelous."-Psalm 139:13,14 NLT

I will admit that this is one of the hardest scriptures for me to believe in the bible; and one of the most difficult thing for me to say is, "Thank you God for my body." This is due to all its deformities. I have a severe clubbed right foot that makes my right leg and foot significantly smaller than the left side. I was born with a dislocated hip, scoliosis, and a missing chest bone. In my opinion after my hair and face, my body goes downhill.

I am also left with scars on my foot, leg, and back as doctors made attempts to correct the way I was "knitted together in my mother's womb." It is very difficult for me to understand how a God who carefully created creation seemed to have missed a few steps while creating me. Of my mother's four children, I seemed to carry the physical deformities for everyone. No one else was born with a physical deformity. For years, I did not question it. However, I would be lying if I said there was never a day I found myself envious of my siblings "normal" bodies and disgusted by mine.

At the age of 12, I pronounced a life sentence of shame and hiding upon my life. I stopped wearing clothes that would reveal what I hated most about me. I stopped wearing sandals because I no longer felt like explaining my condition to people. I did not want pity or sympathy. I just wanted to be normal. So, I became a hider. Into the closet I went, hoping to never have to face those legs of mine again. I thought if I hid them, they would eventually go away. Now that I am almost 31 years old, I can say that was the dumbest idea ever in the history of Charity's dumb ideas. I literally signed my life away when I decided to start hiding. I stopped swimming. I did not try out for any dance team or cheerleading squad because it meant I would have to show my legs. I almost quit softball one year because I thought they were going to make me wear shorts. I removed myself from any activity that required your legs or feet to be seen.

As God would have it, the one activity I could continue was dancing at my church. Our attire was always long and covered! The only thing that gave me assurance that God meant to put me in this body is that even with my deformities, I am still able to dance. Some of my moves are limited, but I can dance unto His glory. He gave me a voice, and I use it for his glory. He has given me the gift of counsel, wisdom, and writing. I use them all for his Glory. The interesting thing is nothing about my physical deformities have stopped the gifts of God from operating through me. The only thing that has hindered those things at any time have been my mind. I have allowed the "what ifs" to keep me from enjoying life. What if my legs become a meme? What if the men who follow me find out and stop following me? What if people start treating me with pity because they discover the truth?

I never considered what if you share your story and help others overcome their own insecurities? What if your process of freedom convinces others to find freedom? What if God placed you on this earth as an example that people are only limited by their mind not by their deformities? Today I began my pursuit of Freedom, and my prayer is by the end of this journey through the wilderness of my soul I will be able to say, "Thank you for making me so wonderfully complex! Your workmanship is marvelous!!!"

FREEDOM QUESTIONS:

1. What made you purchase this workbook?

2. If the reason is because you desire Freedom in your soul, are you willing to be honest with yourself concerning the things that entangle you?

3. What is the thing(s) that keep you from living in freedom?

4. What is the thing that you find most difficult to accept about yourself?

5. How could your story help others once you have healed

from the wounds of the past?

6. What would a life of freedom look like to you? Describe it in detail. It will be your motivation to stick to the next 39 days of your life.

FREEDOM PRAYER:

Dear God, I need you to dig deeply into the depths of my heart and shine your light of truth on its darkness. I need you to confront every lie, deceptive, seductive, and manipulative way found at the core of me. I am asking for freedom. Free me from the chains of my past. Remove the sting of past life events. Comfort the areas of my heart that mourn the loss of loved ones, missed opportunities, and moments of failure. Create a heart of flesh from this surrendered stony heart of mine. Refine me in your fire and mold me on your Potter's wheel. I rejoice that when you are done, I will be convinced that I am a new creation in You! Thanks for everything! Amen.

DAY 2
Ticking Time Bomb

I never sedated my emotions I simply suppressed them. I did not smoke weed, pop pills, or be promiscuous. I chose a different poison. I immersed myself into work; fixing other people's problem; and getting into relationships solely to have that euphoric feeling that comes with being a new couple. I depended on the issues of others to keep me distracted from own feelings. I will admit that it was twisted, and it created unhealthy relationships.

You become their "go to" person for everything that goes wrong in their life. Then, you begin to feel an obligation to become their problem solver. Although you hate hearing their problems, your ego enjoys being stroked by their praise for fixing them. You become known as the "fixer" to everyone who knows you, and you subconsciously pursue relationships with people who "need" you. This is all kinds of dysfunctional, but this is how you have learned to survive emotionally. You live for euphoria, and you suppress anything that would force you to come down from it.

People always assume you are great because of your ability to fix things. They never ask about your day, and they never take a moment from themselves to help you. Since you have learned this to be the case you are lonely and internally sad. You have learned to keep face and fool the crowd; but your soul is screaming for attention. Your hurts long to be addressed. Your fears want to be expressed. Your regrets are waiting to be acknowledged. Your failed attempts at things you really wanted needs your attention. Your heart is torn, damaged, and stony in areas; and ignoring it is no longer working. Your emotions have now become a ticking time bomb waiting for the most inopportune time of your life to explode and cause damage beyond your capacity to fix. Before it happens, I encourage you to take the brave step with me and examine your heart. Take the next 38 days with this book and stop the bomb from exploding. This will start out feeling like death, but it will end in new life. Your soul will finally be free.

FREEDOM QUESTIONS:

1. Describe your current emotional state?

2. What events have occurred in your life that has brought you to this place emotionally?

3. Would you describe yourself as a "fixer" or are you always the broken one?

4. When did you become the fixer, and what do you enjoy about that position in people's lives? What do you dislike about it?

5. When did you become the broken one, and what do you enjoy about that position in people's lives? What do you dislike about it?

6. How long will you tend to the wounds of others and neglect your own?

7. How long will you make people responsible for fixing your problems instead of fixing them yourself?

8. Will you commit the next 38 days to paying attention to your soul and defuse the bomb that is ticking inside of you?

FREEDOM PRAYER:

God, I bring my heart to your throne. I am emotionally exhausted from trying to fix everyone's problems. I have allowed my identity to be wrapped up in people's need for me. I am now in need of your care. I have neglected my own heart trying to tend to the needs of friends, family, etc. Holy Spirit my soul needs to be revived. I have nothing else to give anyone, and I need your help before my neglect causes me both emotional and health problems. Thank you for hearing my prayer. Amen

DAY 3

The Cover Up

The serpent was the shrewdest of all the wild animals the Lord God had made. One day he asked the woman, "Did God really say you must not eat the fruit from any of the trees in the garden?" 2 "Of course we may eat fruit from the trees in the garden," the woman replied. 3 "It's only the fruit from the tree in the middle of the garden that we are not allowed to eat. God said, 'You must not eat it or even touch it; if you do, you will die.'" 4 "You won't die!" the serpent replied to the woman. 5 "God knows that your eyes will be opened as soon as you eat it, and you will be like God, knowing both good and evil." 6 The woman was convinced. She saw that the tree was beautiful and its fruit looked delicious, and she wanted the wisdom it would give her. So, she took some of the fruit and ate it. Then she gave some to her husband, who was with her, and he ate it, too. 7 At that moment their eyes were opened, and they suddenly felt shame at their nakedness. So, they sewed fig leaves together to cover themselves. 8 When the cool evening breezes were blowing, the man and his wife heard the Lord God walking about in the garden. So, they hid from the Lord God among the trees. [9] Then the Lord God called to the man, "Where are you?"[10] He replied, "I heard you walking in the garden, so I hid. I was afraid because I was naked."[11] "Who told you that you were naked?" the Lord God asked...-Genesis 3:1-11

Since the Garden, Satan has been cunning in seducing mankind into sin. Like Eve and Adam, curiosity about the forbidden lures us into the arms of people and places that leave us naked and ashamed. In an instant, we go from innocent to guilty of sin. Instead of confessing our faults to God, we look for "figs" to cover up. This idea of trying to fix ourselves without God's help is the response of most of us when it comes to sin. We do all we can to cover up our sins and wonder why we feel ashamed in His presence. There is no real human solution for dealing with sin outside of salvation, confession, and repentance. We cannot do as Adam and Eve and blame everyone around us. We must acknowledge what we have done and take responsibility for our choice to sin. Once we have confessed, we must turn away from the thing(s) that have placed us in this sinful predicament. It is the only way fellowship with God can be renewed. We cannot get away from it, and if we refuse to do it, shame will always be the result.

Today I want to invite you on a journey to surrender your "figs," those things you use to cover up you fears, insecurities, guilt, and shame to God. I want to encourage you to discover the joy of renewed fellowship with God by no longer hiding. You have spent years trying to cover up who you really are to the One who knows you best; and today would be a great day to start the process of living a shameless life. God wants the real you, and he wants you to trust Him with the things you continue to hide in hopes no one will see. Your figs can no longer cover you. It is time to allow God to clothe you in his love, forgiveness, and freedom.

FREEDOM QUESTIONS:

1. Adam and Eve used "figs" to cover themselves after disobeying God, what are some things you have used to cover up your sin(s)?

2. In the story, everyone is blaming someone else for their actions. When you fall prey to temptation do you blame others, or do you take responsibility for your choice to yield to it?

3. As a child of God, do you find yourself feeling ashamed or refusing to spend time in His presence because of the things you have done?

4. If so, make a list of the things that keep you "hiding" from God.

5. Looking over the list you made, have you confessed those things to God? If not, how long will you allow guilt and shame to separate you from a renewed relationship with your Creator? Friendly Suggestion: Now would be a great time to confess your sins to him.

FREEDOM PRAYER:

God, please forgive me for trying to hide who I am and what I have done from you. I confess that I ____ tell God what you did , and I take full responsibility for my part. I repent for trying to use the things you created to cover up the sin I committed against you. I would like to begin a new relationship with you, and I desire to know what it means to be loved, forgiven, and free. I recognize that I am incapable of covering me, but I thank you for the Grace you have provided that does it for me. Amen.

DAY 4
The Inclusivity of the Gospel

For everyone who calls on the name of the Lord will be saved!"-
Romans 10:13

Before you freak out, this is not my Coming Out Speech in support of The Gospel of Inclusion. It is simply my little exhaustive list of what the Apostle Paul meant by the word "everyone" in Romans 10:13. I believe this scripture reveals the love, equality, and mercy of God to mankind. Everyone is welcomed to receive salvation if they so desire it. There are no prerequisites. There are no background or credit checks. Your I.Q. is not taken into consideration. Your family history does not keep you from it. Your past is not held against you. Everyone means EVERYONE.

It does not matter if you are liberal or conservative. It does not matter if you are a democrat or republican. It does not matter if you voted for Trump or Clinton. It does not matter if you watch Fox News or CNN. Salvation is yours if you call on the name of the Lord.

It does not matter if you were once a Satanist. It does not matter if you grew up in a Muslim home. It does not matter if you were once a Buddhist. It does not matter if you were once Hotep. It does not matter if you were a Voodoo priest or priestess. It does not matter if you were Wiccan or you worship St. Lucia. Salvation is yours if you call on the name of the Lord.

It does not matter if you enjoy telling little white lies or large white lies. It does not matter if you have found yourself to be a thief, gossiper, and a cheater. It does not matter if you have had an abortion. It does not matter if you have a proclivity towards pedophilia, pornography, homosexuality, or bestiality. It does not matter if you are murderer, rapist, or what most consider to be the lowest of humanity. Salvation is yours if you call on the name of the Lord.

I will admit it took me a while to be comfortable with the idea that everyone can receive salvation. It was only a problem because in my humanity I considered some sins greater than others; but in His divinity, God sees them all the same. He provides the same remedy for every sin we find ourselves entangled in, and that is SALVATION! God never intended salvation to be so complicated. It has always been a matter of simply confessing Jesus as Lord and Savior of your life; and anyone who believes and confess is a recipient of this wonderful Salvation. It is available to "EVERYONE WHO CALLS ON THE NAME OF THE LORD!" Let us stop making Jesus so unattainable to people. Let us keep the Gospel message as simple as Jesus made it in John 3:16, "For God loved the world so much that he gave his one and only Son, so that everyone who believes in him will not perish but have eternal life." (New Living Translation) It really is as simple as believing in Christ and confessing him as our Savior. I pray that this will be the Gospel we share with others. It is really the only one worth sharing!

FREEDOM QUESTIONS:

1. Are you a Christian? Why or Why Not?

2. Do you find it difficult accepting that salvation is available to everyone? Why or Why not?

3. In the writing, I admitted I used to consider some sins greater than the other. Do you have a Hierarchy of Sin list? If so, write it out.

4. Romans 6:23 says, "For the wages of sin is death, but the gift of God is eternal life through Jesus Christ our Lord." If all sin has the same punishment (death), why do you make one sin greater than the other?

5. Now that you know all sin has the same punishment, how does that change your view about who can be saved or not?

Note to the Unbeliever: The ability to obtain freedom from my past started with me accepting Jesus as my Lord and Savior. 2

Corinthians 5:17 says, "Therefore if anyone is in Christ, he is a new creation. The old has passed away. Behold, the new has come!" This book is an opportunity for us to accept what has passed away in order enjoy the new creation we have become. You are under no obligation to be a Christian to complete this book, but I do want you to keep in mind as you read that Salvation is available to you if you want it.

FREEDOM PRAYER:

Thank you God that Salvation belongs to anyone who calls on the name of the Lord. Thank you that when I decided to accept Christ I became a recipient of eternal life. Forgive me for making the Gospel message so complicated and show me how to share it with others. Thank you for the amazing gift of Salvation. May I spend the rest of my days living in gratitude of the kindness you have shown me through Jesus Christ. Amen.

DAY 5
God Where are You?

For since the world, no ear has heard, and no eyes has seen a God like you, who works for those who wait for him."–Isaiah 64:4

At this present moment life appears to be working against me, and I feel like I'm in a holding pattern waiting to land in a beautiful place. I was in dire need of encouragement and this scripture provided it. After reading it, all I could do was pray "Holy Spirit teach me how to rest while I wait for you."

As I uttered that prayer, Isaiah 26:3,4 came to mind. It says, "You will keep in perfect peace all who trust in you, all whose thoughts are fixed on you. Trust in the Lord always for the Lord God is the eternal Rock." Before I could finish writing that verse out to encourage myself, Proverbs 3:5,6 started to flow from my heart and out of my mouth. It says, "Trust in the Lord with all your heart; do not depend on your own understanding. Seek his will in all you do, and he will show you which path to take."

It suddenly clicked that it is in "Total Trust" I find rest while waiting for God. What is Total Trust? It is the complete surrender of our hearts and minds to the faithfulness of God. Total Trust is where we exchange the pride of life for his Presence. It is where we yield our anxiety for His peace. It is where we cast our cares at his feet and bathe in his Love. Total Trust is the place where we surrender our limited knowledge and take rest in his Omniscience. It is where we yield our worry to bask in the beauty of his Sovereignty.

As believers, God made it possible for us to go through the worst of life's trials with "peace that surpasses our understanding." We will never tap into that peace if we keep our minds on everything other than Him. Our focus on Him amid tribulations is what determines whether we rest in Him or become consumed by circumstances.

Today I pray we choose to rest in Him. I pray we choose to turn our focus on the ETERNAL faithfulness of our God instead of the temporary reality of life. I'm not asking that we pretend that life does not hurt at this moment, but I am encouraging us to focus on the Truth of our Father's love instead of the facts of life. When it is over we will look back in awe of His provision, and we will laugh at how stressed out we were about the situation.

I encourage us to skip past the worry this time and fast forward to worship. God is going to perform His word over our life, and I pray we take rest in that truth. God loves us; and this trial is another opportunity to learn how to rest while waiting for God to come through. I pray we learn the lesson this time. Isaiah already told us God "works for those who wait for Him." Hang in there, the Father is working for you.

FREEDOM QUESTIONS:

1. What are the things in your life that are stealing your peace?

2. How has worrying helped you to overcome the situation you are facing?

3. How would trusting God help you in this situation?

4. What is keeping you from trusting God with this time?

FREEDOM ASSIGNMENT:

Take a moment and write down all the times you can remember God working things out for you. Once you have made a record of those things keep it as a reminder of God's faithfulness to you. Look over it every time worry tries to come to steal your peace. Once you come out victorious in this battle, add it to the list of things God has worked out for you.

FREEDOM PRAYER

Father forgive me for allowing anxiety to rob me of the peace you have provided. I ask that in this moment of my life that you show me how to please you. I admit this situation has caused me to become weary in waiting for answers. Today, I ask that you help my unbelief and restore my faith. I choose to trust you. Amen.

DAY 6
Teach Me How to Live

"Teach me how to live, O Lord. Lead me along the right path, for my enemies are waiting for me. -Psalm 27:11

Righteous is not just our eternal state, but it should also be our constant pursuit on earth. As believers, we should long to go in the direction that pleases God. Our prayer should be as David to the Lord, "Teach me how to live. Lead me along the right path." However, unless the Holy Spirit teaches us we will be led away by our own desires. David's request to the Lord reveals his humility. He recognized that true righteousness comes from God. He realized God's help was needed to live righteously. He concluded that he did not possess the knowledge on his own, and he had to go to The Righteous One to learn how to live.

David was also aware of the many paths one could take, and he inquired of the Lord to lead him along the right path. We too must acknowledge the different paths in life, and who or what is leading us down them. For example, success is your destination, but you can choose hard work as your vehicle or you can cheat your way to it. Hard work will provide you with success and peace at night. Cheating your way to it may provide you with success, but you won't have peace with it. I pray you choose the right way every time, even when the wrong way appears quicker and easier.

The last thing David points out is he knows his enemies are waiting for him. Let us be clear that as king and commander of the army, David had real enemies. They wanted to physically kill him. They wanted his influence, wealth, and kingdom. Majority of us will never know those kind of enemies, but we do have different temptations, appetites, and selfish ambitions that will lead us astray if we are not careful. Therefore, like David, we must cry out "Teach me how to live. Lead me along the right path. "

Here are some ways he leads us along the right path:

1. His Word. The Bible is the Believer's manual for life. For us, the New Testament reveals the way we should conduct our lives as proof that God lives in us.

2. Personal Experience. There are times that God will allow us to go down a certain path to teach us the right way. If we fail the test, there will be a retake at some point in our life.

3. Prayer. Oftentimes, taking a moment to pray before the decision-making process can keep us from the wrong thing. I would encourage us to converse with God

throughout the day.

4. The Experiences of Others. The Bible is filled with a plethora of "what not to do" stories. It shows us the consequences, so we will not have to experience them. The life lessons of those around us can keep us on the right path if we heed to them.

5. Listening. Taking time to hear the answer can save us years of regret.

In this life many paths and voices will be presented to us. Some will appear good and end up evil, and others will appear scary and end up amazing. I encourage each of us to keep David's words in our hearts. We can never go wrong asking our Creator to lead us along the right path.

FREEDOM QUESTIONS:

1. In the reading, we discussed how the word of God keeps us along the right path. How often do you read your Bible? Is your reading experience enriching or boring? Why? **If reading the Bible is difficult to understand, I encourage you to find a Bible Translation you can understand. **

2. What was the last lesson that you learned from personal experience? Was it a lesson that you failed to learn in the past or was it a new lesson?

3. How often do you pray before making a decision? If you answered, "never," how has that worked for you?

4. Are you a person who learns from other people mistakes or do you tend to only learn lessons through personal experiences? If you must learn by personal experience, how much pain have you experienced by your unwillingness to listen and learn from others?

FREEDOM ASSIGNMENT:

The only way we will be able to learn from the word is by reading it for ourselves. If you do not have a devotional time set in place, I encourage you to read one Bible verse a day for the rest of this challenge. I recommend Psalms 119:9-44 to get started.

FREEDOM PRAYER:

Lord teach me how to live and lead me on the right path. Increase my discernment so that I can know the difference between Your voice and the enemies of my soul. If I am taking the wrong route, please guide me to the right path. Help me to be open to your leading from this day forward. Amen

DAY 7
Nothing is Worth Your Soul

"For what profit is it to a man if he gains the whole world and lose his own soul? Or what will a man give in exchange for his soul?" -Matthew 16:26

In Christendom, this text is often used when trying to persuade someone to avoid "worldly" pursuits. It is used when we are trying to help the Church musician resist the temptation of playing in the club. It is used to convince the Praise leader not to try out for "The Voice." It is a great deterrent in getting people to avoid what we consider Secular ambitions.

We are often so quick to discourage others from doing things outside of the church; but what if the world some of us are trying to gain is the Church? How devastating would it be to bring people to Christ, and you never experience Him? How humiliating would it be to see the one you prayed for welcomed into heaven, and you are unwelcomed? How heartbreaking would it be to discover those you sang for are welcomed, but you are considered unknown by God?

"What profit is it to a man if he gains the whole world and loses his own soul?" The result would be the same as one who never came to know Christ. You spent years selling Salvation, but you never tried it for yourself. The interesting thing about God is he knows our heart, and He knows if we only became a pastor out of our need to be in control versus a genuine love for his people. God knows if we only attend Church out of family tradition versus true dedication to Him. He knows if we play for the church solely for the paycheck versus us worshiping him. God knows if we are a first lady because of the prestige or because we love God, our husband, and the people God has called him to shepherd. God knows if we are the praise leader out of fear of not making it in the secular industry or because our heart's longing to sing for Him.

The bittersweet part of heaven will be those in attendance. Many of us will come before the Lord only to realize we were working for Him, but he never knew us. He never had our hearts. We lived for the Church, for the people, and for the fame. We were devoted to our gifts instead of the Giver. We pledged allegiance to teaching the Bible, but we never submitted our lives to the principles of it. We sold deliverance, but we never sat down long enough to allow God to deliver us. We managed to save the whole world and lose our soul in the process.

I would recommend that every believer take time out to do a soul evaluation, motives maintenance, and a quality assurance check!

It would be robbery for you to never experience the private life changing power of God while preaching it to the public. Stop studying to save everyone else and allow God to seal the areas of your life that need to be saved. Take a sabbatical and pour the issues of your life at His altar. Stop working for the world of Church and get in tune with what God wants from you. God does not want to be your employer, he wants to be your everything.

FREEDOM QUESTIONS:

1. What is your definition of success?

2. What material things do you need to acquire to feel successful?

3. Have you ever considered compromising your morals or abandoning your faith to gain success, fortune, etc.? Why or Why Not?

4. If you attend and serve in your local church, why do you do it?

5. Do you serve in your church to be a blessing to others or because you like to be seen and praised?

6. If your answer was to be seen and praised, how does that honor God?

7. Matthew 7:22,23 reveals how those who gained the Church and lost their soul will be greeted on judgment day, "On judgment day many will say to me, 'Lord! Lord! We

prophesied in your name and cast out demons in your name and performed many miracles in your name. 'But I will reply, 'I never knew you. Get away from me, you who break God's laws.'" How does the thought of being rejected by God after spending years "serving" him make you feel?

8. Do you have a genuine relationship with God? If you answered, "yes," how do you know? If you answered, "no," salvation is available to you today. Ask him to come into your heart and be Lord of your life.

FREEDOM PRAYER

Father help me to stop working for you and teach me how to love you. Forgive me for being more committed to my gifts, my church, and my programs than you. I long to be known by you, and I yield my life to the process of that reality! I repent for worrying about the world and neglecting knowing you. Teach me how to love you better. Amen.

DAY 8
Finding Delight in Him

"Take delight in the Lord, and he will give you your heart's desire." Ps 37:4 (NLT)

When we exalt God above everything, he in turn provides all we need. This principle is made plain in Matthew 6:33, "Seek the Kingdom of God above all else, and live righteously, and he will give you everything you need." (ESV) God should be first when it comes to our pursuits. He must be the number one thing that brings our hearts delight. Anything before him would be considered an idol.

IGod does not do well with idols, and he will crush each one that fights for His position (Exodus 20:4,5; Isaiah 42:8). God delights in blessing his people; but we, his people, must take delight in Him. He must be the most important thing in our life. Everything we do should reflect His righteousness. Everything we say should bring Him praise. Whether we are speaking of Him or speaking to others. The way we talk should honor him.

I know the idea of everything we do must honor Him can be overwhelming for some of us. So, before you break out in hives consider these scriptures:

"For God is working in you, giving you the desire and the power to do what pleases him."-Philippians 2:13

"For I can do all things through Christ, who gives me strength." -Philippians 4:13

God in his kindness never requires something of us that he has not already given us the ability to give or do. We can delight in Him because He provides us the grace to do so. Today, instead of striving to please God in your own strength, receive the grace that He has made available to you. Pleasing God is not impossible, but it requires God to help us do it. I am praying you choose to receive the grace to delight in God so that he can provide you with the desires of your heart. Those desires eventually become quite simple. You find yourself wanting more of Him.

FREEDOM QUESTIONS:

1. Being honest with yourself, what is your greatest desire or delight? Why?

2. If you were to obtain that desire, how would your life change?

3. Does the thing you desire draw you closer to God?

4. Are the things you desire temporary or eternal? Will

obtaining these things produce an everlasting joy or joy for a moment?

5. What would be the benefit of making an eternal God your delight?

6. Does knowing that "God gives you the desire and the power to please him" takes the pressure off you feeling incapable of pleasing Him? Why or why not?

FREEDOM PRAYER

God, there are a lot of things competing for my attention. At times, I am guilty of pursuing the things of this world and neglecting what pleases you. I repent for choosing what is temporal over what is eternal. I thank you for the grace to delight in you with all my heart. I thank you for the balance in pleasing you and enjoying life. Amen

DAY 9
Just Ask!

This morning I woke up, and the conversation I had with my ex-boyfriend replayed in my mind. I had told him I was headed to the library to print some papers off. Thinking I had a printer at home, he said, "Why are you going to the library? You could have bought a printer if you needed one Charity" I told him, "You gave me your card in the event of an emergency. I did not consider a printer a necessity." He sighed and said, "If you wanted the printer all you had to do was ask! You have my card to get what you want." I said, "okay and tried to talk him out of the reasons why I did not need one." Slightly frustrated he said, "the money is there, and I won't be bothered whether you take it or not. You're the one that needs the printer." We laughed and moved passed that part of the conversation. As I thought about our conversation, I realized as it pertains to the things I need, I treat him as I treat God. I would rather not ask him for the things I want.

I know this will sound extremely prideful, but I do not like feeling helpless and asking for assistance. I developed a disdain for asking for help watching and hearing my mom ask others for it growing up. They would often remind her of the last time she asked for help, or they would talk about her needing assistance. My mother was a working woman, with four children, and a seasonal, crack addicted husband. He would play dad for a few weeks, and he would go to do whatever he pleased months at a time. She was often left with the responsibility of everything.

Hearing her ask for help and seeing the sadness in her face after being denied, did something to me. It made me ashamed, and I never wanted to give someone that kind of power over me. I never wanted someone to feel my success, survival, or needs being met was in their hands. I saw asking for help as a sign of weakness, and I never wanted to give people the satisfaction of knowing I was weak. The world is not kind to those who are in need. The world does not care to hear about the story that brought you to the point of need.

I did just fine with this mentality as long as I had a job. It provided me independence, and I did not need anyone's assistance. This gave me power, and it proved I was quite capable of taking care of myself. Now that I am unemployed, I am at the mercies of those who are willing to help. I cannot receive anything without asking for it! If I may be honest, I fear the word "No." I fear the rejection of having my request denied. I fear feeling helpless. I fear being vulnerable. I fear being judged and seen as weak, ignorant, or poor. I have spent all my life trying not to be a beggar. I have prided myself on living as a piper if it kept me free from asking for anything.

I remember growing up and never telling my mom I had outgrown my shoes. I would walk around with too little shoes until she discovered I needed another pair. She always asked, "why didn't I tell her?" and I would say, "I did not know" but I did. I did not want to hear her say "no" or have to borrow money from someone. She had two other children at the time, I cared more about them having what they needed. I will admit that kind of pride can cause physical pain. Shoes that are too small are a pain to walk in. LOL

At this moment, I must let the truth sink in that I have been living in fear and pride for majority of my life. I have allowed the fear of being rejected or denied keep me from asking for the things I want or need from others. It has interfered in my spiritual life as well. Many times, I felt that God had other request that needed His attention more than I did. I had accepted the lie that God is bothered or weighed down by my request. The truth is He delights in me asking (Matt.7:7; John 13:13,14, 15:6,16:24; James 1:5). These scriptures are proof that as a loving God and creator of my life, he wants me to ask Him for my needs and desires. It does not hurt to ask, and he delights in giving us the things we ask for in His name (Luke 11:13).

The pride, which God hates, came from me looking down on my mother for doing what she had to do. I saw her ability to ask for help as a sign of weakness. I made a pact with myself that I would never become a beggar. This attitude of being too good to ask for help has been more of a road block than an assistance in life. All I can do at this point is apologize to my mom and repent to God. I must apologize for holding a grudge against her and judging her for the way she had to provide for us. I must repent to God for functioning all this time from a place of fear and pride.

FREEDOM QUESTIONS:

1. Do you have a hard time asking God for help? Why?

2. Do you have a hard time asking people for help? Why?

3. Is there anyone in your life that has made you ashamed of asking or receiving help?

4. How has refusing to ask for or receive help effected your life?

5. If you decided to start asking for help today in the areas you need it, how would your life improve?

6. List the areas of your life that you need help.

7. When will you release your pride and start asking for what you need?

8. Is there anyone that you need to ask for forgiveness concerning the way you viewed their life decisions? If the person is deceased, writing a letter can remove the weight from your heart.

FREEDOM PRAYER:

Dear God,

I repent for having a proud heart against You and my mother. I repent for believing I was above asking for help. I ask that you forgive my haughty behavior; and I repent for idolizing independence instead of being dependent on you. Please forgive me for accepting lies of you being too busy to care about my needs. Thank you for revealing the deception that has jaded my view of you, others, and myself. Today, I choose humility, and I will make my request known from this day forward. I am not above anyone, and everyone deserves to be respected whether they are the lender, borrower, or beggar. Thank you, Holy Spirit for revealing the truth about who I really am, and who you desire me to become. Continue to reveal every contradiction, hypocrisy, pride, and false humility in my heart that would get in the way of my love for you, others, and myself. Today I choose to walk in love, and I receive your perfect love that casts out all fear. I have nothing or no one to fear. Thanks for exposing my dirty laundry, and thanks for purifying my heart with your truth and love. May my life be a testament of your love, grace, and truth in Jesus name. Amen

DAY 10
Short and in need of a Savior

"He tried to look at Jesus, but he was too short to see over the crowd. So, he ran ahead and climbed a sycamore-fig tree beside the road for Jesus was going to pass that way."-Luke 19:3,4

Standing 4'11 with no assistance from heels, I can relate to Zacchaeus's issue of being too short to see someone. He was a chief tax collector in the region, and he wanted to see Jesus. He was not going to wait for someone to assist him. He did not say, "oh I am too short, I will never see Jesus." He did not wait for permission from anyone to run ahead. Instead he solved his own problem despite his physical limitation. The bible tells us, "he ran ahead and climbed a tree." Wait a minute! A grown, business man, sat his age and status to the side and reverts to child-like behavior to see Jesus?

Zacchaeus, small in stature, and big in faith was committed to his goal. He was relentless, and he refused to be denied. The desire to see God caused him to become innovative and use the resources around him to get what he wanted. A tree that was typically used for shade, bearing fruit, and a jungle gym for children had become a stepstool or ladder for Zacchaeus. His faith, innovation, and persistence not only fulfilled his desire, but it yielded a reward. Zacchaeus only desired to see Jesus, but what Jesus saw was a true son of Abraham in Zacchaeus.

He did not just get to see Jesus, but he was able to dine with him. Jesus wanted to be a guest in his home. I am almost certain he was not prepared for such a request, but he obliged. The request was twofold. It was an invitation to his house and heart. It was no secret that Zacchaeus was a notorious sinner (v.7), but his response in v. 8 reveals his repentant heart, "I will give half my wealth to the poor, and if I have cheated people on their taxes, I will give them back four times as much." Before Jesus and the crowd, he acknowledged the thing that made him sinful. He committed himself to being both compassionate by giving to the poor and integral by paying back those he cheated. He had to acknowledge his wrong before allowing Jesus into his heart. Verses 9 and 10 gives Christ's response and the opinion of the crowd did not matter. Zacchaeus had been accepted by Jesus, and he was given the honor of having dinner with the King!

Zacchaeus is a reminder that our shortcomings, no pun intended, do not matter to God. He sees our faith beyond our faults. It would behoove all of us to have the tenacity of Zacchaeus when it comes to seeing Jesus or reaching our goals in life. DO NOT ALLOW ANTYHING TO STOP YOU. Do not allow your natural limitations to be the reason you quit. Find your tree or that thing around you that will allow you to see like everyone else. Zacchaeus stood out because he was hanging on a tree. Maybe Jesus saw himself when he saw Zacchaeus, and he knew that he would soon bear all his sins on a similar tree to the one Zacchaeus was seeing him from, who knows?

Zacchaeus used what was around him to get what he wanted, and you must do the same. Remove the limitations so that you can become innovative. There is something, someone, or some place in your vicinity that has the solution to having the desire of your heart met. Revert to child-like solutions if you must, but get it done by any means necessary.

Do not worry about your past. It cannot be the reason why you talk yourself out of the possibility of your future. Ignore the crowd! There will be plenty of people who will know about your previous reputation, and they will feel you are disqualified. DO NOT LISTEN! Your name was called not theirs! God's grace and your faith got you there not your previous experience or past reputation. You may receive more than what you desire. DO NOT TALK YOURSELF OUT OF IT. Instead, do what is necessary to adjust to what is being asked or required of you. Your real identity is revealed when you answer the call of salvation or the call of your dreams. Who you really are comes to the surface when you do what you are born to do. Find that tree so that you can see yourself the way God sees you Zacchaeus.

FREEDOM QUESTIONS:

1. What are the things that you consider to be limitations

in your life?

2. What is it that you desire to do?

3. What are the resources around you that can help bring that desire to pass? (Think like a child).

4. If you received the desire of your heart right now, would you be prepared to properly maintain it?

5. If you answer was no, what are some things you could be doing now to better prepare you for what you desire?

FREEDOM ASSIGNMENT:

Using the answers from Question 5, create a plan to complete all the things in your listed. If research is required to find assistance, start researching. Do not let anything stop you from doing what you are able to do. I truly believe that God will meet you where your faith is and go beyond what you expected. Get to work Zacchaeus, your opportunity will be passing by shortly.

FREEDOM PRAYER

God I repent for allowing what I have considered limitations in my life to keep me from you. Forgive me for always making excuses as to why I cannot be or do what you ask of me. Today, I choose to chase after you like Zacchaeus! I will not allow anything to stop me from having a relationship with you. I thank you for the mind of an innovator. I will no longer look at my environment as an obstacle but an opportunity to create another route for others to follow. Like Zacchaeus saw the tree as a tool to get closer to you, show me what I can use that will draw others closer to you. Amen.

DAY 11
Watch Your Step

"Truly God is good to Israel, to those who hearts are pure. But as for me, I almost lost my footing. My feet were slipping, and I was almost gone. For I envied the proud when I saw them prosper despite their wickedness."-Psalm 73:1,2

I would like to believe I have read every Psalm in the book of Psalms, but today I am not so sure. I can relate to the psalmist much more than I would like to here. I wish I could be one that could say I have never envied the wicked. I wish I could say I never pondered, "why do they prosper when they do wicked things?" I wish I could say I have never questioned, "what is the purpose of living righteous when it appears that God allows the wicked to prosper?" I too almost slipped into an unclean heart as I was slowly but surely allowing envy to consume it.

Even in my own family, it appears that those who know God suffer financially, while those who could care less about righteousness have all the latest and greatest of things. Even the few of them that are unemployed appear to live better than some of the Christians in my family. Seeing that does something to your psyche especially growing up under the Word of Faith doctrine. Being told "the wealth of the wicked was stored up for the righteous" made me envious. This envy in me simultaneously invited two other visitors to my unclean heart, jealousy and entitlement.

Jealousy evokes feelings of anger. Envy caused feelings of discontentment and resentful longing for someone else's possessions, qualities, and good fortune. I was not just discontent with my life in comparison to theirs, but I was angry about it. This jealousy and envy in my heart made me miserable, bitter, and an ungrateful person. Here I am serving God; rejecting propositions to do something strange for some change; staying away from the club; and walking away from an opportunity to do what I love because I would have to compromise my morals to obtain it; and I still must deal with lack in my life? I have to live paycheck to paycheck. Where does God get glory in that? How does my life appeal to those who have everything they want?

Then, I had an encounter with the Holy Spirit that reminded me of the covenant I am under and who I am serving. He reminded me I am considered a Gentile, and the covenant God made with the people of Israel DOES NOT BELONG TO ME! God allowed Israel's covenant to be one of riches and wealth if they kept his commands. It was necessary for them to have many possessions so that the nations around them would fear their God. He gave them all the possessions their world had to offer, but their hearts continually strayed from him. The more they acquired, the more they would stray.

Knowing the pattern and tendency of man to serve what they possess instead of God, he revised the covenant. In the redemptive plan to save all of mankind, he changed the covenant from a physical one to a spiritual one. There was no more promises of material things, but the promise of an eternal relationship with Him. There was a promise of being part of a Kingdom that the wealth of the earth could not be compared to it. There was a promise of spiritual fruit rather than a land flowing with milk and honey. This covenant secured our salvation forever. We no longer had to participate in sacrifices because the greatest sacrifice had been given for our lives. I had to stop desiring a covenant that was not mine and accept the one that belongs to me.

It was in that moment that my desires shifted. I stopped longing for the riches of this world and started longing for the wealth of God's kingdom. I began to long for what was eternal versus what was temporal. I started to see the Big Picture, and that is "I'm living for eternity, and what I do here will set me up in Heaven." I may not gain the wealth of the wicked, but I will obtain the reward of the righteous. I may not get the fancy cars and homes while sojourning through this land; but my estate in Glory will be eternal. I had to remember I am living for eternity whereas the wicked is living for the day. I do not have to envy their possessions because they won't be able to take them. They will be left for someone else to enjoy, but I'll have many rewards awaiting me in Heaven. That's Good News!!!

FREEDOM QUESTIONS:

1. Have you been guilty of being envious of unbelievers?

2. If yes, what was the reason(s) you envied them?

3. In the reading, I discussed that Israel possessed a different covenant than the New Testament believer. Are you aware of which promises are yours according to your covenant? If yes, list them. If no, please read the entire book of Romans to understand the New Covenant between God and man.

4. Does understanding your covenant is a spiritual one help you not covet the wealth of the wicked? Why or Why Not?

5. Who shaped your philosophy about money? Do you see wealth as a good thing or evil thing?

6. Do you believe that being or appearing wealthy is the only way to get the attention of unbelievers? Why or Why Not?

7. If God never blessed you with another material thing in your life, would you still be willing to serve Him for the rest of your days?

8. If the unbeliever has worked for the wealth they have acquired, why do you think some Christians feel that prayer alone will produce wealth for them?

FREEDOM PRAYER:

I repent for being envious of unbelievers. I have spent many days angry and bitter at their success in comparison to my struggles. I repent of having a lazy faith that assumed prayer alone makes me eligible for the wealth of this land. Today, I ask you for the wisdom on how to acquire wealth, and I thank you this time I will work to obtain it. I also thank you for bringing me into a greater understanding of the covenant I have with you according to your word. Bring to light every place I have been deceived or taught incorrectly concerning it. Thank you so much for your love and grace towards me. Amen.

DAY 12
The Cost of Looking Back

"But Lot's wife looked back and was turned into a pillar of salt." Gen 19:26

Who would have ever thought a simple glance behind you could forfeit everything in front of you but such is the tragedy of Lot's wife. The instructions were clear, and their new place of residence was determined, Genesis 19:17 says, "...run for your lives! And don't look back or stop anywhere in the valley. Escape to the mountains or you will be swept away." They were headed to the mountains; getting ready to embark upon a great adventure; and while running for their lives, Lot's wife becomes salt. Before we cast a stone at the Salt lady, let us consider ourselves. How many times has looking at our past caused us to become bitter and unable to move forward into the future? Lot's wife was disobedient when she turned to look back, but can you blame her for desiring one more peak at the city that was once her home? I, like Lot's wife, have been guilty of revisiting my past sometimes whether it has been with an old boyfriend, old hangouts, or a drink I used to enjoy.

What is so appealing about our past that causes us to return there so easily? Is it because it is comfortable? Is it because it is familiar? Is it because we are afraid of what is ahead? Or are we just too lazy to face the obstacle the future may present (i.e a greater anointing, a new mate, job, business, etc.)? My question is why couldn't Lot's wife let go of her past? Maybe she considered all the time she invested into making her old city a place her family could live. Maybe investing the time to establish a new home in a new city, was too overwhelming for her. Who knows? But the tragedy of it all is that the one thing she thought she could not do without caused her death, made her stiff, and incapable of experiencing her future. This has happened and is happening to many of us.

My challenge to each person that reads this is to let go of those things that are behind you! Nothing your past has to offer is worth the expense of your future!!! I know this is easier said than done; but trust me it is worth it in the end. Giving up everything, including our past, is a part of being a disciple (Luke 14:33). It may be hard but remember "with Christ all things are possible!" Trust that God is capable and well "able to keep you from falling" back into your past. Although this walk with Christ maybe difficult at times, the rewards of it are eternal!!!

FREEDOM QUESTIONS:

1. What is the thing(s) in your past that is extremely hard for you to let go?

2. Why do you feel such an attachment to the person, place, or thing?

3. Is this person, place or thing worth your future?

FREEDOM ASSIGNMENT:

Write a letter to someone who is struggling with the same thing you are facing. In the letter, be transparent about your struggle; provide encouragement to overcome the struggle; and provide practical ways to assist in letting go of that thing in their past. Once you have completed the letter, read over it and start following the advice you so graciously gave another in your situation (smile).

FREEDOM PRAYER:

God help me! I have a sick fascination with the things of my past. I tend to find myself reliving certain memories in my mind. I cannot seem to leave the people from it. I seem to be obsessed with the old me and the things I used to do. I ask that you help me move forward. I need your strength to do it. Living in the past is robbing me of my present and future. I want to experience what it means to be a new creation in you. Today, I choose to look towards you and the life you have in store for me. Amen.

DAY 13
Getting What You Want From God

Have you ever had trouble getting things from God? Have you found yourself frustrated with seeing people receive the things you have been requesting? If you answered, "Yes" to those two questions I have a few suggestions for you. Here are three fireproof ways to get what you want from God:

1. Delight Yourself in Him. In Psalm 37:4, King David spills the beans on his success. He says, "Take delight in the Lord, and he will give you the desires of your heart." David was encouraging the reader to take pleasure in pleasing God. By doing so, God will give you the desires of your heart. When he becomes our delight he simultaneously becomes our heart's greatest desire. It gives God great pleasure to be our greatest treasure.

2. Watch What You're Doing. Psalms 84:11 says, "For the Lord God is our sun and our shield. He gives us grace and glory. The Lord will withhold no good thing from those who do what is right." The Psalmist wrote this in light

of his personal experiences with God and the experiences of the children of Israel. Throughout the Old Testament we see this principle in action. Every time the children of Israel did what pleased God, things were great for them. They conquered nations. They had the best land. They acquired the spoils of war, and they lacked no good thing. But as soon as they opted to please themselves and walk in unrighteousness, the good life turned into a miserable one. There were famines, diseases, and death in the land. They were conquered by nations that once feared them. They were forced into exile; and the things they desired ultimately insured their demise. Knowing these things David wisely concludes, "do what is right." Do the things that please God. Keep His commandments before you and rid yourself of what dishonors Him. By doing this, God will graciously give you what is good for your life.

3. Prioritize. In the middle of delivering a prolific sermon, Jesus summarizes a portion of it by saying these words in Matthew 6:33, "But seek first his kingdom and his righteousness, and all these things will be given to you as well." If you take the time to read the entire chapter, you will discover that he was speaking of those things that causes most of us to worry or sin trying to acquire. In this verse, Jesus reveals our greatest need and shares the formula for Kingdom success without asking for an offering. To know God is the greatest need of every person on this earth; and pursuing righteousness should be top priority

in every Christian's life. If we want what is in God's hand, we should first desire what pleases His heart. Dedicate your life to what honors Him and everything else will fall in place.

The purpose of writing this was to encourage you to give God what He desires from you. We could spend a lifetime trying to acquire things and never find fulfillment; or we can commune with the Giver of life and always be fulfilled. Everything you need is in knowing your Creator. If we find the time to know God's heart, he will graciously give us all we need and more.

FREEDOM QUESTIONS:

1. Being honest with yourself, what are your three greatest desire in life?

2. Did God make the list?

3. If your greatest desire was fulfilled, do you think you would be fulfilled forever or will you eventually desire something else?

4. Describe your relationship with God. Do you talk to him often or only when you need something?

5. Is your relationship more about what you can get from God or what you can give to God?

6. Describe what it would be like if God treated you the way you treated him. Considering your description, if you were God would you give you the desires of your heart?

7. What are some things you can do differently to improve your relationship with God?

8. Knowing that God gives you the grace to please him (Philippians 2:13), when are you going to start giving more of an effort to pleasing him? I hope your answer was today.

FREEDOM PRAYER:

God, forgive me for making my pursuit after you about me. I repent for allowing selfish desires to lead my pursuits. Show me the parts of my life that do not honor you. Grant me strength to pursue what pleases you the most. Today, I commit to loving you because of your goodness and not my greed. Amen.

DAY 14
It Will Cost You

The disciples were astounded. "Then who in the world can be saved?" they asked. ²⁶Jesus looked at them intently and said, "Humanly speaking it is impossible. But with God everything is possible."-Matthew 19:25,26

As a kid, the story of the Rich Young Ruler used to be a sad story to read. I felt that it was so unfair that he walked away feeling as if he could not inherit Eternal Life. I always thought Jesus was a little harsh with the way he handled the young man until I paid close attention to the attitude of the rich ruler. His initial question in Matthew 19:16 (NLT) was "what Good deeds must I do to have eternal life?" This idea of physically doing something to get something from God is the way of the Law, and this is why Jesus gave him a response that suited his mentality (Matthew 19:18-21). In Christ's omniscience, he knew the commandments the Young Ruler was keeping, but he demanded of the man that which was most important to him, his riches. It was at this request that the rich ruler did not see eternal life obtainable in His own strength. He walked away feeling unfit for Eternal Life because He had to give up the thing that defined his life. However, those who stayed with Jesus received a revelation about Salvation. In verse 26, Jesus says, "Humanly speaking [salvation] is impossible. But with God everything is possible."

In two sentences, Jesus revealed the exhaustion that comes with keeping the Law, and the grace that comes from receiving God's gift of salvation. Jesus wanted people to see that human efforts do not make salvation possible, only God does! This was the same thing Paul was reiterating to the Church of Ephesus in Ephesians 2:8,9, "God saved you by his grace when you believed. You cannot take credit for this; it is a gift from God. ⁹Salvation is not a reward for the good things we have done, so none of us can boast about it." Salvation is a gift from God, and there is nothing we can do outside of believing in our heart and confessing with our mouth that he is Lord to obtain it.

If you need more proof, I Corinthians 1:30, 31 will provide it, "God has united you with Christ Jesus. For our benefit, God made him to be wisdom himself. Christ made us right with God; he made us pure and holy, and freed us from sin. 31 Therefore as the scriptures say, "If you want to boast, boast only about the Lord." Our salvation comes from God alone, and the only human that will ever be able to boast about their works saving anyone is Jesus. If we for a moment assume that we have done such great deeds to stay saved or become saved, we are like the Rich Young Ruler. You will also come to a point where you realize your human efforts will never be enough, and you will be left with the option of walking away or clinging to Christ, Our Righteousness. My prayer is that you will be found clinging to Christ. Salvation is a beautiful thing when you rest in the truth that it is all God's doing from START to FINISH (Hebrews 12:2)! I pray you rest from the law and start to live in the grace that Jesus finished the work that was necessary for you to be in right standing with God.

FREEDOM QUESTIONS:

1. In the story, the Rich Young Ruler valued his possessions over a relationship with God. What are the things in your life that make you walk away from serving God wholeheartedly?

2. What is your most prized possession on this earth? If God asked it of you, would you give it to him for the prize of Eternal Life? Why or why not?

3. Jesus revealed that Eternal Life cannot be obtained by human efforts but through God alone. Does this Bible truth contradict or agrees with what you have been taught in Church?

4. List the things that you have been told that you must do to be saved besides "believe and confess that Jesus is Lord."

5. Compare the things you listed to what I Corinthians 1:30,31 and Ephesians 2:8,9 says about what makes your salvation possible.

6. If you are aware that God makes pleasing him possible, what is stopping you from giving all of who you are in exchange for what he has in store for you?

7. Can God have your greatest possession in exchange for the gift of righteousness He has given all who believes in Jesus?

FREEDOM PRAYER:

Father I have tried in my own strength to be righteous, and I am exhausted. Today, I surrender my human efforts and I receive the work that Jesus Christ did for me. I will no longer wonder about my salvation because I rest in truth of my righteousness is in Jesus. I thank you that I no longer live right in hopes of staying saved, but I pursue righteousness because I am saved. Today, I will receive the salvation you have made available to me, and I will live in the freedom of that truth. Amen.

DAY 15
The All Sufficient One

Today I was spending time preparing for speaking engagement entitled "Mask Off." I began to pray that the masks would come off me first. As I started to study the text a Song of Deliverance came to me. Here are the lyrics:

There is nothing missing, lacking or broken in you. Your love heals. Your love delivers. There is nothing missing, lacking, or broken in you.

I cannot explain the freedom that occurred as I played the song back. For many years I have felt that something was missing from my life because of the absence of my father. I felt I was always lacking because I was raised in poverty. I felt broken because I was convinced no one would want someone that was molested; abandoned by her father; grew up in poverty; and born with physical deformities. I have always felt like being me was not enough, and I was unworthy of love. Why would anyone, including God, want to love me, bless me, or like me?

Today God reminded me that he is El Shaddai, the All Sufficient

One. I searched for a definition for "all sufficient" and found one from www.answer.com to be pretty cool. It says:

All sufficient means being able to care for the needs and hopes of others as well as yourself without being disorganized as well as doing everything and anything without mishaps in anything and is only possible for a super-being such as God.

All that I need is found in El Shaddai. There is nothing missing, lacking, or broken in those who have been raptured by God's love. His love is perfect. It brings wholeness to the areas we feel are missing. It picks up the slack and fills the void of areas in our life that feel empty. The love of God mends the broken places, and it casts out all fear. El Shaddai, God Almighty, provides all we need and is the Source of life itself. If God Almighty was able to create the universe, he can make our life whole.

FREEDOM QUESTIONS:

1. Do you feel that there is anything missing, lacking, or broken in your life? If so, list them.

2. Why do you feel that way about those things?

3. Does knowing that God is All Sufficient bring any hope to your heart concerning the areas you mentioned?

4. What is the thing(s) that make it difficult for you to believe that God, as your Creator, delights in being the source of all you need?

5. Have you ever felt unworthy of God's love, attention, or

concern about you? Why?

6. What would a life of wholeness look like to you? How would it feel? How would you think? What would you look like? How would you act? Describe it.

FREEDOM ASSIGNMENT:

Keep what you wrote for number 6 as road map in the direction you are headed in life. Screenshot, type it out, or whatever you need to do to have it near when your past or people suggest that place is not possible for you. Keep it as a prayer before the Lord, and trust that El Shaddai is the greatest source and resource that you have in this life.

FREEDOM PRAYER:

Father thank you for reminding me that there is nothing missing, lacking, or broken in You. Forgive me for trying to find other sources for acceptance, affirmation, and completion. Today, I rejoice in you being El Shaddai in my life. I thank you for guiding my path to the people, places, and things that will help me. Amen

DAY 16:
El Roi: The God Who Sees Me

One of my favorite names to use for God when praying is "El Roi." Every time I use it I find it to be an instant reminder that He is aware of my circumstances. It tends to ease the ache of my heart; and it places my focus back on his promise to never forsake me. In Genesis 16, we are introduced to the name El Roi, by a woman named Hagar. For those of us who may not be familiar with Hagar, she was the servant of Sarai (Abram's wife). Sarai had the bright idea to help God in fulfilling His promise to her husband and suggested that Abram sleep with Hagar. As Sarai desired, Hagar became pregnant. Once pregnant Hagar started to treat Sarai with contempt (v.4). Sarai returns the favor and treats Hagar so harshly that she runs away. It is in this time of running that she is found by the loving-kindness of God:

The angel of the LORD found Hagar beside a spring of water in the wilderness, along the road to Shur. [8]The angel said to her, "Hagar, Sarai's servant, where have you come from, and where are you going?" "I'm running away from my mistress, Sarai," she replied. [9]The angel of the LORD said to her, "Return to your mistress, and submit to her authority." [10]Then he added, "I will give you more descendants than you can count."[11]And the angel also said, "You are now pregnant and will give birth to a son. You are to name him Ishmael (which means 'God hears'), for the

LORD has heard your cry of distress. [12]This son of yours will be a wild man, as untamed as a wild donkey! He will raise his fist against everyone, and everyone will be against him. Yes, he will live in open hostility against all his relatives." [13]Thereafter, Hagar used another name to refer to the LORD, who had spoken to her. She said, "You are the God who sees me." She also said, "Have I truly seen the One who sees me?" [14]So that well was named Beer-lahai-roi (which means "well of the Living One who sees me"). It can still be found between Kadesh and Bered. [15]So Hagar gave Abram a son, and Abram named him Ishmael. (New Living Translation)

In this story, I find the timing of God very interesting. At any moment, He could have revealed himself. However, he waits until Hagar is expecting and in a dry place before He reveals he has been with her the entire time. He waits until she is out of options, without friends, and without any sense of direction before he says, "I see you!" He allows her to feel every ounce of fear, isolation, and abandonment before revealing the "I AM" is with you. It took her being away from all she had ever known to experience God for herself.

God did not simply reveal himself to her in the wilderness; but he spoke to her purpose. He provided her with instructions on how to rectify her past mistakes (v.9); and he gave her insight to what her future would entail (vv. 10-12). It never ceases to amaze me how one encounter with God can bring wholeness and clarity to the thing that pains us the most. Hagar heeded to the instructions that were given to her, and she was able to return "home" with a better understanding of who her God was and what was in store for her future.

For those of us who may be in a wilderness situation like Hagar, I would encourage us to:

1. Sit still for a moment and allow the voice of God to speak to our situation.

2. Admit where we were wrong and mishandled the situation, relationship, etc.

3. Stop rehearsing the offenses and choose to forgive those who hurt us.

4. Obey the instructions that God gives us.

5. Walk free from condemnation knowing that the God who sees has come to our rescue.

El Roi is aware of all that is hurting you, and he is waiting for the moment that you stop trying to figure things out. He longs to commune with you so that He can reveal the truth of who he is and who you are to him. My prayer is that you come to know God as El Roi, the God who sees me so that you can see yourself as He does. Hagar's life was never the same, and I am certain when you encounter him your life will change.

FREEDOM QUESTIONS:

1. Have you ever been considered a threat and ostracized by people who once cared about you? Describe how it made you feel.

2. In that moment of being mistreated by people, did you ever feel abandoned by God?

3. During Hagar's time in the wilderness, she discovered something new about God. What lessons about God and yourself have you learned during your wilderness experience?

4. Did God give you any instructions about your purpose or how to resolve the situation? Have you obeyed his request as Hagar did?

5. How does it make you feel to know that God sees you the same way he saw Hagar in her pain?

6. Oftentimes when we are in isolation, the enemy will try to tempt us with bitterness, unforgiveness, and condemnation. Is there anyone that you need to forgive? List their names.

FREEDOM PRAYER:

El Roi thank you for keeping your eyes upon me. Thank you for coming to my rescue and showing me that my past offenses do not disqualify me from fulfilling my purpose. Today, I release the offenses of my past, and I choose to forgive those who have hurt me. Amen

CONFRONTING YOURSELF:

Build me an altar with your life as the sacrifice. Surrender everything! Place all of who you are on it that I may consume every part of you that is not of me. Stay still for the purification and allow my Word to cleanse you. You have given your time and energy to everyone else. Now it is time to give your time and energy to knowing who you are in me. Your freedom is contingent upon you receiving my forgiveness concerning your past. Acceptance of who you are will only happen when you realize who you are in me. You will never live in love until you entrust me with your fears, failures, and pain. I long to heal your heart, but you must first lay yourself on the altar as a living sacrifice. It is where the desires of your spirit will be manifested and others will come to see you have changed through me. I am ready when you are!

-Your Creator

DAY 17:
My Heart

Broken, shattered, disfigured, abused. The love that is to be found there has been misused.

Past experiences have caused a cement wall around it, and an electrical fence smacked dead in the middle of it.

Wanting to love freely, I constantly contend with my past. To let go sounds easy, but the reality of this is a tedious task.

Disappointment and abandonment have been the crutches I have held on to: wanting to let go but so confused on how to.

I hear that you love me and won't fail, but my heart is finding that truth difficult to receive. Considering it is only acquainted with the agony of mistrust.

If I may be honest, the beat of my heart is doubt. How can I trust you?

I have placed my trust in those who you sent only to be disappointed.

To see you as a father is more painful than seeing you as a friend. If my earthly father is an example of who you are, I'd rather not have a part of you!

God, I greatly desire to trust you and be loved by you, but I am afraid if I do you will eventually hurt me too!

But in this matter, I am compelled to ignore what my heart tells me to do. Father in all sincerity I am afraid to love you, but I want to.

I have some inhibitions leaning on my intuition, but considering your ways are not like man, maybe just maybe I can try this me loving you and you loving me thing! God just do not fail me because you are my heart's last resort.

I wrote this poem January 29, 2007 at 3:15am. It was a couple of months before I decided to go see a counselor, and I was in a bad place emotionally, spiritually, physically, and financially. I was tired of having my heart broken by men; sick of being disappointed by Christians; and I was over sowing any seeds towards anything that had to do with a church. My heart had become both a maximum-security prison and a chemical plant full of toxic waste. I meant every word of the poem. I was at a crossroad of either find something more concrete about my Christian faith or walking away from it. Today let's explore the condition of your heart. Answer the questions honestly. If you are a Christian, do not be afraid of expressing where you are and what you feel. God already knows, and he has been waiting on you to be honest with him.

FREEDOM QUESTIONS:

1. Describe the condition of your heart right now?

2. List the things that has caused it to be the way you described it.

3. I mentioned in the poem that I have a problem trusting God because of my experience with others. Are there any concepts about God that you wrestle with because of what others have done to you? If yes, please list them.

4. What are your thoughts concerning Christianity? Is there any teaching that has turned your heart bitter towards the Faith? List them.

5. What are your thoughts towards people? Do you like them? Are you suspicious or afraid of them?

6. When you are alone, what are some of the thoughts that come to your mind concerning your identity?

7. The next part of this book will focus on the issues of your heart, and it will require full disclosure in the presence of God. It is the only way we can find freedom and obtain a new heart. Are you ready to exchange your old heart for a new one?

FREEDOM PRAYER:

Father I can no longer carry this broken heart of mine around. I am tired of pretending like I'm not hurting. I have spent years trying to love you and others in my own strength, and I am exhausted. I need a clean heart. I need one that is free from the pressure of religion and clear of the pain of my past. I surrender my heart, and I receive the one your love produces within me. Amen.

DAY 18:
A Deceitful Truth

The heart is deceitful above all things and desperately wicked; who can know it? -Jeremiah 17:9

Yesterday on Twitter I tweeted, "If living "your truth" is sin in the sight of God, you are still living a lie. As Christians, the Bible always trumps our truth." I followed that tweet up with "satisfying your flesh is bliss until the enemy comes to collect, and sin is always paid in death. #Romans 6:23" I know death sounds extreme, but it is true. Consider a thief and the instant gratification that comes with acquiring that stolen object; however, once the thief is discovered he will either experience death to his freedom or his life. Consider the adulterer, he enjoys the moments of pleasure with his lover, but once his infidelity is discovered it leads to the death of his marriage or life.

You may be wondering, Charity what does that have to do with living "my truth?" I'm glad you asked. Oftentimes, living our truth comes at the expense of clinging to sin. Especially if our truth is being with another man's wife; cheating your customers; etc. Usually our "truths" are lived from our hearts, and that is a dangerous place to acquire truth. Matthew 15:19 says, "For from the heart comes evil thoughts, murder, adultery, all sexual immorality, theft, and slander." In other words, "it is deceitful above all things and desperately wicked." Even as Christians, we risk the chance of being led astray by the suggestions of our heart.

Christ admonished us in Matthew 22:37 to "love the Lord your God with all your heart..." Jesus knew that if we did not submit to God's lordship in our hearts that our lives would not reflect His presence. Matthew 15:18 says, "But the things that come out of the mouth proceeds from the heart, and this defiles a person." This also rings true about the way we live. If we are living from the truth of our hearts that have not been submitted to God, we will live lives that lead to all kinds of death.

The world has a luxury that we gave up when we decided to become a Christian, and that is the permission to live by their "truth." They have the right to sleep with who they want; marry who they want; and take what they want. We relinquished those rights to obtain the privilege of being children of God. We no longer live according to the truths of our heart, but we live according to the truths of God's Word. "Following our heart" is no longer an adequate excuse to remain in sin. God's Truth, the Bible, trumps the suggestions of the heart.

We must decide to live according to the flesh (the suggestions of our heart) or the Spirit (the suggestions of the Holy Spirit). I encourage each of us to take a moment today and examine the "truths" we are living. If the Bible is clear on the matter, bring yourself under the subjection of God's truth. If the Bible is unclear on the matter, seek wise counsel and be prayerful until you receive instructions on what to do. Always remember living any truth outside of God's word will result in death (Romans 8:5-13). Today I pray we as believers are found choosing life.

FREEDOM QUESTIONS:

1. As a Christian, what truth are you living that is contrary to God's word? List all of them.

2. Knowing your lifestyle is displeasing to God, how do you justify your decision to live your way?

3. Considering the truth found in Matthew 15:19, how often has your heart led you astray to live a truth contrary to God's word?

4. John 14: 15 says, "If you love me, you will keep my commandments." As a Christian, does your current lifestyle reflect loving God or loving the world?

5. Romans 6:1,2 says, "Well then, should we keep on sinning so that God can show us more and more of his wonderful grace? Of course not! Since we have died to sin, how can we continue to live in it?" When will you choose to stop being a prisoner of sin and enjoy your new life in Christ?

FREEDOM ASSIGNMENT:

For the next 24 hours, pay close attention the words that come out of your mouth. Make a list with two categories (Matthew 5:18, 19 and Philippians 4:8). If you discover that more vile and wicked things come from your mouth than good, it is time to make some changes to better represent Christ. You can start with repentance. Then, you can follow that up with renewing your mind with the word of God.

FREEDOM PRAYER:

Father thank you so much for the privilege of being your child, and I repent for living a life that does not reflect I belong to You. Today, I ask that you bring to light all the "truths" that I have been living contrary to your word. Today I submit to your lordship over my heart, and I thank you for the grace to live in a way that is proof of your existence in me in Jesus name. Amen.

DAY 19
Dear God

I have so much bitterness, anger, rage, and envy in my heart. I am bitter because of the time I wasted with certain people and pursuits in life. I am bitter about not being married. Why have I not been deemed worthy of being a man's wife? I look at some women who are married; and it baffles my mind that someone would marry them. You put all this love in my heart for someone I have yet to meet and each day feels like torture carrying it around. I'm bitter!

I am angry because of the time and energy I put into others is never poured back into me. No one ever checks on me. No one cares to know how I am doing. No one sends me words of encouragement. I want to be loved and to know it. People say the words, but that is typically after I have done something for them. I am angry at myself because of the time I've wasted pleasing people and longing to be accepted. I have given far too many years to caring about what others think of me. I am angry with you that I was born the way I am. All these damn deformities and no one else in my family have them. I have felt like a weirdo all my life because of them. I try to pretend it does not bother me, but I find it to be absolutely unfair. What did I do to deserve this? Why do I have to carry this burden? To add insult to injury, I have a love for shoes, and I have been created in a way that I am unable to wear the kind I love. God it's not fair, and I hate being this way. I'm angry!!!

The rage comes from refusing to acknowledge the areas of bitterness and anger in my heart. I feel as if I am ticking time bomb. Like someone is going to ask me for something, and they are going to catch everything I have been wanting to say all this time. I hate to admit it, but God I am full of rage.

I am envious. It stems from my desire to be married. Those who I have considered my closest friends are married with families of their own, and I too desire that in some form. I want the companionship. I want someone I can build with and help see our dreams come true together. I want a person I can confide in and make love to as my husband. I want someone that I can share all parts of my life with and know that I am safe with him. I confess I am envious.

God as I have honestly stated the things that fill my heart, I ask that you remove the bitterness, anger, rage, and envy. I repent for holding on to these feelings for so long and allowing them to reside in a place that was meant for your dwelling. I cannot make any progress in life holding on to resentment; clinging to the past; being angry about things that are beyond my control;

and envying what others possess. Today I pray that as I have confessed the true condition of my heart, you are now able to remove what is toxic, repair what is broken, and fill it with your truth and love. Today I release the things that have hindered my progress so that I can move forward in the things of You. Thanks for revealing what I could not see in Me.

Forever Grateful,

Charity Israel

FREEDOM ASSIGNMENT:

Write an honest letter to God about the condition of your heart. Tell God the truth, the whole truth, and nothing but the truth. Do not try to say what you think God would like to hear, but tell him where you really are at this moment of your life. You will never be free to enjoy life until you start speaking the truth about who you are and where you are. Admit where parts of you take delight in indulging in sin. Admit where you have held an offense against God, his people, and even yourself. This letter is between you and him. There is no judgement in confession. After you have made your Confession Statement, write a prayer from your heart.

FREEDOM PRAYER:

God your word tells me in I John 1:9 that "If [I] confess [my] sins to [you], [you] are faithful and just to forgive [me of my] sins and to cleanse [me] from all wickedness. Today, I have shared with you the truth about my heart, and I thank you for forgiving me and cleansing me from all unrighteousness. I give my heart back to you, and I thank you for teaching me how to guard it with all diligence in Jesus name. Amen.

DAY 20
Me, Myself, and My Lying Lips

"Save me Lord from lying lips and from deceitful tongues."-
Psalm 120:2

It makes sense to ask God to keep you from the lies and deceit of others; but what if your tongue is the one causing all the harm? Before I could say "amen," about protection from other people's lies, I was reminded of the lies and deception my lips were guilty of spewing. I was notorious for a little white lie or a hyperbole to get people to think I was more than what I was. As I considered how I fabricated stories in scaring people into receiving Jesus, I had to repent. I have lied about my family life in hopes of fitting in with others. The more I think about it, a liar would be a good word to describe me based on my frequent tendency to exaggerate the truth. I painted pretty pictures to others so that my mind could cancel out the ugly truths about my life.

Lying became my way to escape from the harsh realities of home. I did not lie to get out of trouble. I did not lie to acquire material things. I lied in hopes of being loved and accepted. Telling the truth would have meant accepting my circumstances, and I was not interested. However, I had to admit that I possessed lying lips and a deceitful tongue.

Wow that felt good to get off my chest. I am now free to tell the truth. I am no longer ashamed. My past does not have to be something that I attempt to avoid. I can go back and reclaim the freedom I allowed a lie to take from me. This task will not be easy. However, if what I am feeling in my heart is any indication of the liberty to come, I must keep walking this way. As I started to consider what a life lived in truth would look like a question came to my mind, "What will I have to hold on to if I let go of the lies?" The Holy Spirit replied, "Love and truth!" What more could one need in this life?

FREEDOM QUESTIONS:

1. Do you ever find yourself lying or exaggerating about things in your life?

2. What makes a lie more appealing than telling the truth for you?

3. Do you consider yourself a liar?

4. Do you feel guilty when you lie or have you become such a master of it that your conscience has been singed?

5. What truth(s) about your life are you hiding from others?

6. What truth(s) about your life have you exaggerated in

hopes of being accepted, loved, etc.?

7. Have you considered surrendering your lying lips and deceitful tongue over to God in exchange for His truth and love? If so, what is stopping you from doing it?

Freedom Challenge: For the next 21 days commit to telling the truth. You will need it to complete this book. When we lie the first person we deceive is ourselves, and we will never find freedom in telling and living lies. I pray you take the challenge one day at a time. Habits are hard to break, but with God as your strength you will overcome this one.

FREEDOM PRAYER:

Your word says in Proverbs 12:22 that "The Lord hates liars but is pleased with those who keep their word." Father I repent for my lying, exaggerating tongue. Forgive me for using lies to deceive people into thinking I'm someone I am not and exaggerating stories in hopes of receiving their approval. Today, with the help of the Holy Spirit, may I become a person who is obsessed with seeking and telling the truth. Knowing that you have a great future in store for me, may I be a person that accepts the truth about my past and present situation. Amen.

DAY 21:
The Power of Confession

Finally, I confessed all my sins to you and stopped trying to hide my guilt. I said to myself, "I will confess my rebellion to the Lord." And you forgave me! All my guilt is gone."-Psalm 32:5

For the last few days I have been meditating on this scripture; and reflecting on the many times that I wanted to live in rebellion rather than experience redemption. I remember the countless times I tried to justify certain thoughts, behaviors, and motives. I can recall the plethora of times that I lingered in sin a little longer than I should have and the consequences that accompanied such dumb life decisions.

Once I started to get serious about my relationship with God honesty became a requirement for it to function properly. As I began to spend time in prayer and studying scripture, sin was not so easy to commit or leave unconfessed. The magnitude of His love compelled me to tell the truth about me. I could no longer pretend that the life I was living was one that pleased Him. I had two options: to live a lie and remain outside of his presence or to start confessing so that I could fully enjoy His presence. Like the Psalmist I said to myself, "I will confess my rebellion to the Lord."

I John 1:9 tells us "if we confess our sins to him, he is faithful and just to forgive us our sins and to cleanse us from all wickedness." As I did this I began to experience freedom from guilt, shame, and public opinion of my past. Assurance in God's forgiveness produces freedom. However, we will NEVER know that freedom if we choose to remain in rebellion and unconfessed sin. We will spend our time trying to justify our actions to ourselves and to those around us. Even worse we will become reprobate and sever our relationship with God. He never leaves us, but we will leave Him as we allow both shame and pride to keep us from confessing what we have done. One of the most cunning weapons of the enemy is to convince us that we have done too much wrong to receive the love and forgiveness of God; and I am here to tell you that as the "Father of Lies" that is one of his greatest lies!!!

The truth of the matter is "God showed his great love for us by sending Christ to die for us while we were still sinners. And since we have been made right in God's sight by the blood of Christ, he will certainly save us from God's condemnation." (Rom. 5:8,9) There is no sin, outside of blaspheming the Holy Ghost, that will keep you from the forgiving grace of God. If he sent His son while we were in sin, surely any sin we have committed is forgivable if we are willing to confess it. Do not allow the enemy of your soul or even yourself talk you out of receiving the freedom from guilt that is made available to us through confession.

God sent Jesus so that we could have the opportunity to have a relationship with Him. Do not let the moments of slipping or even falling into sin keep you from experiencing the beauty of having a relationship with your Creator. He gave us an anecdote for renewing our relationship with Him after we have fallen prey to the sin. Confession is the key, and it is a blessing to those who will humble themselves and tell God the truth. I pray from this day forward you will choose to confess instead of cover up. You will never have peace inside until you reconcile your relationship with the One who made you, and confession makes it possible. I pray you will find the time to do it.-

FREEDOM ASSIGNMENT:

CONFESS YOUR SINS BEFORE GOD. Don't make excuses for it. Do not try to justify it or make it sound good. Tell God the truth about the things you have done in your life. Stop allowing the enemy of your soul to keep you in shame and guilt. Stop allowing your flesh to keep you in condemnation. Your refusal to acknowledge the sin you have committed and are committing is what has caused a rift in your relationship with him. Today free yourself by way of confession. He is waiting and willing to forgive what you request. If you are unsure of what sin entails read Romans 13:13, 14.

FREEDOM PRAYER:

God I recognize that there are areas in my life that displease you. I have tried to ignore the sins I have committed against you, but I can no longer live in fear, shame, or condemnation. Today I confess these sins before you, and I thank you for forgiving me of them. Amen

DAY 22
Confession of a Broken Heart: God I Hate You

Yesterday, I wrote a letter to myself. Towards the end of the letter I wrote, "Release your doubt. It is interfering with you trusting in God." As I looked at the words "trusting in God," anger started to rise in me. The thought of trusting Him again made me furious. Just a few weeks ago, I called myself trusting God, and I felt extremely humiliated because of it. I was at a Women's conference. During one of the sessions a woman was ministering, and she said, "There are three women here with one of their legs shorter than the other and as a result you have back problems. Come up here, God is going to heal you."

I have not responded to an altar call for healing in years because people tend to blame your faith when it is not manifested. However, no one had been as specific as her. I thought it would be wise to make my way up there. As I was at the altar, I said, "God this would be an awesome moment to heal me. There are a thousand people here, and it would be a great moment for you to get the Glory. I'm here in faith, and I trust in you to heal me."

The minister gets to me, and she has me sit in a chair. She pulls both of my legs up, and you can see that one of my feet and legs are extremely smaller and shorter than the other. She gets on her knees and begins to pray and pull at my leg. After a minute or so of praying, she tells me, "I have been healed because at first she couldn't feel a part of my foot that she could feel now." I politely told her, "nothing has changed." She tried to tell me again, "Oh yes I saw it." I told her, "I have been believing God for this for over 32 years. No one wants it to be true more than I do, but nothing happened." She then tells me, "well keep believing" and walks off to the next person. According to everyone else that went up for prayer they were healed; but I had to take the walk of shame back to my seat. I sat there feeling like the worst practical joke ever was played on me.

God already knew where I was in my faith. He knew I came there needing to be restored, and that moment made everything in that conference null and void to me. I had to fight the urge to run and not come back for the rest of the conference. Everyone went on as nothing happened. My roommate tried to console me, but I was too hurt to cry about it. I decided to retreat to the theologian in me and convince myself everything was okay. I went to the back of the church, and I danced as an act of faith that shame would not consume me. I completed the conference, and I headed back home feeling worse than when I arrived.

Yesterday, the suggestion of trusting God pissed me off! Trust him for what? Lately, trusting Him has resulted in disappointment. Trusting him has resulted in great loss for me. As I thought of all the times I went up for prayer; believed for something; or was required to give something these words flowed from my lips, "God I hate you!" I started to confess "God I hate you created me this way and permitted the deformities I have. I hate that you made me the daughter of a man that was fine abandoning his children. I hate that you allowed me to be born into a family plagued with poverty and procrastination. I hate that I have lived righteous for you and have nothing to show for it. I hate that you took every man that loved me away from me (my grandfather, Pastor James, and Dean Goldsby)" I went on and on about who, what, and why I hated God.

I could not stop myself. It was in my heart for years. I held resentment towards God about things that happened when I was four and five years of age. I have been trying to love and serve a God that in my inner most being, I did not trust. I gave my life to him at 7. I was filled with the Holy Ghost at 14 and started preaching. I went to college and obtained a degree in Pastoral Care Ministries. I spent three years in a Ministers in Training course and became a licensed minister at 25. Now at the age of 32, I discover that God has always loved me, but I have never truly trusted Him. It is hard to trust someone when you harbor hate and resentment towards them. I had to sit in the reality of my relationship with God. I had to accept that it was rotting at its core. It was in this moment that I asked myself, "Do I really want to serve God?"

My relationship with God has been extremely self-centered and self-serving. Most of it has been because of bad teaching on faith.

Not receiving something I believed I could "name and claim" caused a lot of unspoken resentment in my heart towards God. Hearing people say, "all you must do is have "faith," and you'll be healed" caused much disappointment each time I walked away from the altar the same. Believing that "the wealth of the wicked is laid up for the righteous" and battling poverty made being righteous comical to me. All my life, faith has been taught to me as something I must possess to get what I want from God. However, scripture says the opposite. Faith is something I must possess to get God's will accomplished (Hebrews 11). I have spent the last 24 years of my life subconsciously pursuing God's hand and not his heart.

Yesterday, the Holy Spirit tended to the garden of my heart, and he uprooted the weeds that were choking out my true faith in God. By the end of my prayer time, I found myself weeping, repenting, and committing my life to God's definition of faith. Now the cry of my heart is truly God how may I serve you? I have spent 24 years trying to get God to line up with my will for my life. I at least owe him 24 years of lining my life up with His will. LOL This truth pill was extremely difficult to swallow, but I am grateful for it. It is only a reminder that God loves me, and that he is fully invested in completing the good work he began in me (Philippians 1:6).

FREEDOM QUESTIONS:

1. What are your thoughts about what you just read? Can you relate to it?

2. Do you find it difficult to trust God? Why or why not?

3. Considering your life's journey, has there ever been a moment that you felt betrayed by God? How did you handle it?

4. What was the greatest disappoint you experienced as a believer?

5. Did it or has it turned your heart bitter towards trusting God?

6. Has the bitterness caused a rift in your relationship with God?

7. Will you ever admit to God that you have been hurt by some of the decisions He has made according to his sovereignty (death of a family member, a failed business venture, and etc.)?

8. When will you forgive God and renew your relationship with him?

FREEDOM ASSIGNMENT:

Create a list of all the things that you are holding against God. Write out the disappointments, grudges, and moments of shame. Use the list you created and complete this sentence: God I confess that I have been holding _____ against you. Today, I ask that you forgive me for holding this in my heart in Jesus name Amen.

FREEDOM PRAYER:

God, thank you that I can be honest with you in your presence. Thank you that there is nothing in my heart that I cannot express to you. Forgive me for storing bitterness, hate, anger, and disappointment towards you in my heart. I thank you that as I have confessed you have forgiven me. I thank you that my heart can now receive your love and be open to what faith looks like to you. Thank you for your unconditional love, and the freedom it provides. Amen

DAY 23
Hidden Motives

Today during prayer, the Holy Spirit revealed truth about an area in my life. He revealed a 20-year secret that has been my motivation for success and being a "good" person. This secret has been the force behind my academic and social pursuits. This hidden thing has been the motive behind getting involved with certain men. In all honesty, it has been what I have pursued since the age of five. This hidden motivation has been for the approval, acceptance, and awaited return of my biological father. Since the time he has left, I have been on a subconscious pursuit of ensuring his return. I found my niche in academia and tried to excel in hopes he would approve and want me again. I found out I possessed the ability to write, and I thought being a world-renowned author would invoke his presence again. I assumed if I was stylish enough and able to cover up my disability, he would surely desire his beautiful daughter. I have spent seven years trying to figure out what career path would award me the greatest honors and accolades that would deem me worthy of being his daughter.

For the last 20 years my life has been secretly motivated by a desperate need of affirmation, acceptance, and love from my father. The harsh reality is that he may never come back, and I cannot spend my life pursuing things to please a man that willfully chose to leave his children. I can no longer live by this motivation. Living this way has resulted in confusion, disappointment, discontentment, rejection, bitterness, and the list goes on and on. To sum it up, I am unhappy, dissatisfied, and unsure of myself. I have put on a façade of confidence and now at the ripe age of 25, the façade must come to an end. I am tired of putting on, and I desire the authentic confidence of a Holy God to be my portion. For years, I have been a coward on pursuit of approval by others instead of embracing the confidence my identity in Christ provides.

God, I repent for idolizing the approval of my father. I thank you for allowing this day to be the day you confront the true motives behind what I do. Today I remove the idols of approval and success off the throne of my heart. I place the pursuit of your kingdom and righteousness in their place. This day I ask from my heart, "would you, will you, can you be the Father my heart has longed for since my dad left me?" I want to know you as Abba. I need a father in Jesus name. Amen

FREEDOM QUESTIONS:

1. What motivates you?

2. Who motivates you?

3. What is the driving force behind everything you do?

4. Is there anyone in your life that you felt if I had their approval, all would be right in the world?

5. Whose opinion of you have you idolized over God's thoughts about you?

6. Is there anything in your life that you feel you must acquire in order to receive the love of God or man?

7. From a scale of 1-10, what number would you give your level of confidence? Why did you choose that number?

8. Ephesian 1:5 says, "God decided in advance to adopt us into his family by bringing us to himself through Jesus Christ. This is what he wanted to do, and it gave him great pleasure." If you have wrestled with being accepted by your parents, how does it feel to know that it gives God great pleasure to have you as his child?

FREEDOM PRAYER:

God, I repent for idolizing the approval of my father. I thank you for allowing this day to be the day you confront the true motives behind what I do. Today, I remove the idols of approval and success off the throne of my heart. I place the pursuit of your kingdom and righteousness in their place. This day I ask from my heart, "would you, will you, can you be the Father my heart has longed for since my dad left me?" I want to know you as Abba. I need a father in Jesus name. Amen

**I idolized the approval of my father. When you say the prayer repent for what you idolized. **

DAY 24
My Not So Strange Addiction

Every athlete exercises self-control in all things. They do it to receive a perishable wreath, but we an imperishable. -I Corinthians 9:25 (ESV)

Self-control also known as discipline is something I have wrestled with for much of my adult life. Before college everyone told you what to do. Once you turn 18 you are on you own, and you have to figure it out for yourself. For the last 12 years, I have been trying to figure it out. Along the way, due to my lack of self-control, I have acquired certain addictions. I am grateful that none of them have been self-harming such as drugs, alcohol, and sex; but each of them have pulled me away from important things as I freely give them my energy. Who am I kidding? They have been self-harming because they stole my time, and I can never get that back.

The one that has stolen the most of my time is Social Media! I did not grow up with a computer or the internet in my house.

Once I got to college, a whole new world was introduced to me. I started out with Yahoo chatrooms. Then I moved to Myspace and from there Black Planet to Facebook, Instagram and Twitter (kind of). With shame, I admit that much of my college life was spent addicted to Social Media. Since I am confessing much of my life after college has been spent doing the same. I am scared to see the amount of time I have given Facebook. I have been on it for 11 years, and I am certain I have given at least two years in time to it. It may be more, and that is time I will never get back. I convinced myself that it is not that bad considering I have helped people, but the truth is IT'S BAD! It is bad for a few reasons:

1. It has kept me distracted from doing what I was put on this earth to do.

2. It fed my need for attention and validation. Everyone wants "Likes" right?

3. It distracted me from the real world.

Social Media is a pseudo-world that only gets the part of you that you desire to give or for some make up. You in turn want to stay in the world you created leaving the real world to be ignored. With all the time I have given Facebook, I could have earned a couple of degrees by now. Please do not get me wrong. I am not calling Facebook evil, but it has been a nemesis in my life due to my lack of self-control, horrible time management, and my twisted need for validation. It has cost me more than it has ever given me in Likes and Shares. So, for the next 21 days of my life I am signing out of the Social Media world, and I am going to give my time to the things that will ensure I am on the right path for my life. I am going to exercise some self-control and make some moves that matter in the real world. I have some projects that need to be completed. This time away will give me the time to do it. It is said, "It takes 21 days to form a habit," and I am making a habit of spending my time wisely.

Fact of the matter is many of us are addicted to something, and it has robbed us of purpose, time, and moments with our family. It has demanded our undivided attention, and we have come to believe that we cannot exist, live, or function without this substance, person, or activity. The truth is we can live free from the things that entangle us by making the decision to do so! Will it be easy? For most of us it will be the hardest thing we have ever done; but it will also be one of the most rewarding, once we take back our lives!

I am excited about the next 21 days, which started the moment I wrote it. Waiting until tomorrow will give my mind time to talk me out of it, and this is something that must be done! I hope you are brave enough to start today as well. It has been something you have known you needed to quit for a while, and you will not quit until you quit!!! I'm praying for your strength to do it.

FREEDOM QUESTIONS:

1. What are the three most important things in your life?

2. What are the three things that consume most of your time in life?

3. Are the things that take up the most time in your life pushing you towards or away from the three things that matter most to you?

4. If you answered pushing you away, can you do anything to fix the disconnect between what is most important and what has you time? If yes, write it down.

5. The things that take up your time, do you find yourself in a position of being unable to control yourself?

6. An addiction is defined by The American Psychiatric Association as "a chronic disease that is manifested by compulsive substance use despite harmful consequences." Is there anything in your life despite its harmful consequences to your time, family, job, and even yourself that you cannot seem to let go of? Write it or them down.

7. How long are you interested in those things dictating your life? Be honest with yourself here. You may not be ready to let it go, and it is okay to admit it. I would encourage you to go to the next page. If you are ready, what date are you evicting your addiction(s)?

8. What is it about the person, place, or thing that you are addicted to? How does it make you feel? What does it provide? What does it hide about you? What does it validate in you? What does it permit you to escape from in life under its influence?

9. What are some practical steps you can take to rid your life

of what has had you under its control? Be specific because this will become your Emancipation Proclamation for your life.

10. Now that you have created a plan, when do you plan on starting it, cold turkey???

11. Get started!!!

FREEDOM ASSIGNMENT:

DO IT TODAY or start the process of getting help!!! If you need to join a support group, DO IT! There is nothing to be ashamed of about seeking help. It is an act of love to yourself and those you love.

FREEDOM PRAYER:

I thank you that there is no addiction greater than the name of Jesus Christ. I thank you for the grace to live free from every addiction that has plagued my life until today. I thank you that the Cross bore my addictions, and Jesus resurrection secured my freedom from them. Holy Spirit thank you for teaching me how to live a life free from addiction. Thank you for directing me to the places and people that will help me embrace my new life. Every addiction must leave my life in Jesus name, and I thank you for the grace to overcome. Amen

DAY 25

No Time to Waste

"For everything there is a season, a time for every activity under heaven."-Ecclesiastes 3:1 NLT

Dear God,

I don't know how much time has been allotted to me on this earth, but you do. I do know that I have not been a good steward of it. I have wasted it on meaningless pursuits. I have wasted it worrying why am I here, and on what I should be doing. I have wasted it investing into the wrong people, and I do not want to go another day wasting your gift of time. It is the most precious thing, outside of Salvation, that you have given mankind. Forgive me for not appreciating it as I should.

FREEDOM QUESTIONS:

1. Do you value the gift of Time? Why or why not?

2. How have you wasted this gift God has given you? List some of the activities that steal time from you.

3. Why do you give your time to those things?

4. What are some things that you could be doing with your time that could benefit your future?

5. What is stopping you from investing your time in people and things that matter?

6. When will you stop making excuses for where you are in life?

7. How much time are you planning to waste after this moment?

FREEDOM PRAYER:

Today, I repent for not being a good steward of my time. I have made a habit of wasting it, and I need your wisdom to spend it properly. My focus has been on everything but You. I have made my attempts to pursue education, love, a career, and ministry only to have none of those things work in my favor. So here I am depleted, exhausted, and desperate to know, "how do you intend for me to spend my time on this earth?" I am no longer looking for other options. I just want your will to be done in my life. I am ready to serve you with all of me this time. Nothing else is in the way or even desired. Losing everything has proven I can live without everything except you. You are my greatest need and desire in life. I just want to know I'm truly pleasing you, and that is how I will measure my success in this life. I just want to make sure you smile Father! Please show me how! Amen.

DAY 26
Embrace the Waiting Season

But God had mercy on me so that Christ Jesus could use me as a prime example of his great patience with even the worst sinners. Then others will realize that they, too, can believe in him and receive eternal life. -I Timothy 1:16(NLT)

This morning I woke up to a YouTube message entitled "God is Patient" by Priscilla Shirer. During the message she talked about a young woman who felt led by God to leave her great job, and after two years, nothing big had come of it. She had become a babysitter and thoroughly enjoyed it. However, she had become discouraged because she had assumed "greater" would be in the type of job she had and never considered greater being the size of the impact she would make. One day she admitted her disappointment to God. That evening while babysitting, God revealed her significance in that position. As I listened, I could not help but think of my own situation. I left my job as a Flight Attendant believing and knowing I heard God to do so. I left the convenience of a steady paycheck, health insurance, a 401k, and flight benefits. I walked away from it all and six months later I am unemployed and a bit weary.

I have heard so many words concerning International ministry that I have had a hard time coping with the being a "nobody" phase of life. I have been so fixated on getting to the nations that I have forgotten about my neighborhood. I have been sitting around waiting for "ministry" to fall into my lap instead of just ministering to everyone and anyone when I get a chance. Priscilla said something during her message that made me see my present situation from a different perspective. She talked about how the enemy will try to discredit your position in life and will try to make you feel insignificant doing the task that matter most to God. The truth is I am in a great place. I have an opportunity to reinvent life as I have known it; and I have an opportunity to meet the needs of my local community. I managed to forget all about them so concerned about my turn to preach to the "nations." I truly appreciate God for his kind reminder that I am right where he wants me.

FREEDOM QUESTIONS:

1. How would you describe your life at this moment? Is it everything you imagined it would be or does it feel as if you are living a nightmare?

2. Is your present position in life a result of you obeying God's word or disobeying it?

3. If obeying God has brought you to a dry place, how can changing your perspective about your current situation?

4. If living unrighteous has brought you to a dry place, how can repenting and renewing your fellowship with God bring joy back to your life?

FREEDOM PRAYER:

God, I repent for not appreciating the beautiful place you have me now. I repent for allowing my plans to overshadow yours. Today, I release all the prophetic words, selfish ambitions, areas of entitlement, and desires that displease you. Today, I surrender all my ideas of what ministry is. I thank you for choosing me for the task and place that honors you most. Thank you so much for your patience with me, and I thank you for your purposes being fulfilled in my life! Thank you for the ministry of Priscilla Shirer. I needed the reminder of just how patient you are with us in the process of being formed in Your image and likeness.

Day 27: Death's Reminder to Live

Today, I read some bad news on Facebook that took my breath away. A dear classmate was killed in a car wreck. He was such a beautiful soul. He loved to sing, and he was a joy to be around. The news was so devastating because he was a young man. He was only three years older than me. Reading about his death caused me to reflect on my own life. If it had been me instead of him, I would have robbed the world of what I was created to give it. They would not have the books, the music, and gifts inside of me. I have been holding all these things inside of me like I know tomorrow belongs to me. I have allowed someone to hold my heart hostage like I have years to give away. I have been waiting for approval, affirmation, and permission to be great from people who are clueless about their own purpose. I have put off living as if I know when I am going to die. Thank you God for the unwanted gift of death. It's a sobering reminder to focus on what matters. All I want to do is preach the gospel, encourage people to live now, sing, dance, and restore communities. It's time to do it.

FREEDOM QUESTIONS:

1. Are you a good steward of your time and talents? Why or why not?

2. What problem(s) are you created to solve while on earth?

3. List your talents and passions.

4. What life issue (poverty, justice, etc.) or group of people are you most compassionate towards?

5. Write down what your dream job would be? Make sure it incorporates your talents, passions, and the people or cause you want to serve.

6. If you were to pass away today, would you feel confident in knowing you fulfilled your purpose? Why or why not?

7. Who or what is hindering you?

8. How much time do you think you have to put off pursuing what you were created to do?

9. When are you going to stop robbing the world of what you were created to give us?

FREEDOM PRAYER:

God, I am guilty of wasting the time you have allotted me on earth. I repent for squandering my time on meaningless things and unhealthy relationships. Today I ask that you grant me insight into what it is I have been placed on this earth to do. Let me give my attention to things that will have an eternal impact. I am glad that you are a God that redeems the time. With the grace you provide, I will accomplish that which you created me to do. Amen.

DAY 27
Death's Reminder to Live

Today, I read some bad news on Facebook that took my breath away. A dear classmate was killed in a car wreck. He was such a beautiful soul. He loved to sing, and he was a joy to be around. The news was so devastating because he was a young man. He was only three years older than me. Reading about his death caused me to reflect on my own life. If it had been me instead of him, I would have robbed the world of what I was created to give it. They would not have the books, the music, and gifts inside of me. I have been holding all these things inside of me like I know tomorrow belongs to me. I have allowed someone to hold my heart hostage like I have years to give away. I have been waiting for approval, affirmation, and permission to be great from people who are clueless about their own purpose. I have put off living as if I know when I am going to die. Thank you God for the unwanted gift of death. It's a sobering reminder to focus on what matters. All I want to do is preach the gospel, encourage people to live now, sing, dance, and restore communities. It's time to do it.

FREEDOM QUESTIONS:

1. Are you a good steward of your time and talents? Why or why not?

2. What problem(s) are you created to solve while on earth?

3. List your talents and passions.

4. What life issue (poverty, justice, etc.) or group of people are you most compassionate towards?

5. Write down what your dream job would be? Make sure it incorporates your talents, passions, and the people or cause you want to serve.

6. If you were to pass away today, would you feel confident in knowing you fulfilled your purpose? Why or why not?

7. Who or what is hindering you?

8. How much time do you think you have to put off pursuing what you were created to do?

9. When are you going to stop robbing the world of what you were created to give us?

FREEDOM PRAYER:

God, I am guilty of wasting the time you have allotted me on earth. I repent for squandering my time on meaningless things and unhealthy relationships. Today I ask that you grant me insight into what it is I have been placed on this earth to do. Let me give my attention to things that will have an eternal impact. I am glad that you are a God that redeems the time. With the grace you provide, I will accomplish that which you created me to do. Amen.

DAY 28
The Limp

During the night Jacob got up and took his two wives, his two servant wives, and his eleven sons and crossed the Jabbok River with them. [23]After taking them to the other side, he sent over all his possessions. [24]This left Jacob all alone in the camp, and a man came and wrestled with him until the dawn began to break. [25]When the man saw that he would not win the match, he touched Jacob's hip and wrenched it out of its socket. [26]Then the man said, "Let me go, for the dawn is breaking!" But Jacob said, "I will not let you go unless you bless me." [27]"What is your name?" the man asked. He replied, "Jacob." [28]"Your name will no longer be Jacob," the man told him. "From now on you will be called Israel, because you have fought with God and with men and have won." [29]"Please tell me your name," Jacob said. "Why do you want to know my name?" the man replied. Then he blessed Jacob there. [30]Jacob named the place Peniel (which means "face of God"), for he said, "I have seen God face to face, yet my life has been spared." [31]The sun was rising as Jacob left Peniel, and he was limping because of the injury to his hip. [32]Even today the people of Israel don't eat the tendon near the hip socket because of what happened that night when the man strained the tendon of Jacob's hip . -Genesis 32:22-32

Today, I was thinking about the many times I have been ashamed of the way I walk in public. I try to walk behind people using them as a shield. I used them to keep people from seeing my limp. The limp came from being born with a dislocated hip and scoliosis. Over the years, it has become more obvious because of the way I must manipulate my shoes to wear the same size. Considering that I am well acquainted with the discomfort of a limp, I have always been intrigued by this story about Jacob.

I find it interesting that Jacob was given a limp after he was blessed. He was forced to live with a certain discomfort for the rest of his life after receiving the greatest blessing of his life. He lost his ability to walk like everyone else to obtain something others would never receive. He received a new name which was followed up by a new walk. His blessing was a name change which altered his destiny and gave him purpose. He went from a trickster to the victorious one. Verse 28 says, "Your name will no longer be Jacob, "the man told him, "From now on you will be called Israel because you have fought with God and with men and have won." Jacob's life consisted of tricking people. Once he encountered the divine his life changed forever.

Those who knew him before his limp may have felt pity for him, but every time Israel took a step with that foot it declared "VICTORY!" It said the God of heaven says, "you win with

Him and man." It said, "I know your past, and I had to give you a new name so that you could see your future." It says, "it may take you a little longer to get to your destination than others, but you will get there." It is also a physical manifestation of God's grace where death should have been the result. Verse 30, says, "Jacob named the place Peniel (which means "face of God") for he said, "I have seen God face to face, yet my life has been spared." That limp is a reminder of the mercies of God.

Considering this, I must change the lenses I use to I look at my limp. It was predicted that I would not walk, or if I did, I would need braces and assistance for the rest of my life. I was walking by 13 months on my own. By four, I did not need braces to assist me. The kid who was supposed to need assistance walking for the rest of her life is a Liturgical dancer. This limp is not a thing to be ashamed of but a gift to be grateful for. I could be paralyzed or bound to a brace, but I am able to walk on my own every day without assistance. This limp defies doctor's reports. This limp proves God's will trumps the predictions of man. This limp is freedom from braces. This limp is God's grace and proof I WIN with Him and man.

I was so caught up in looking at others in envy that I have missed the moments to be grateful. I have walked in shame when I should be walking Godly proud. Each step I take is proof that God's will supersedes man's predictions. I should be walking unapologetically because it was once said I would not be able to walk at all. This limp means I WIN, and I will not know defeat as long as i'm stepping with God.

FREEDOM QUESTIONS:

1. At this present moment, what is the thing(s) you have been ashamed of that you try to hide in public?

2. How has hiding helped you achieve anything great in your life?

3. What are the excuses you make for hiding your past, flaws, failures, etc.?

4. How could changing your perspective change your attitude and ultimately your life about the thing(s) you try to hide from others?

5. In the reading, I pointed out something that could have been worse than what I am dealing with such as paralysis, wearing braces, etc. Can you find anything to be grateful for instead of being ashamed?

FREEDOM PRAYER:

God, I thank you that there is nothing to be ashamed of concerning my body or life experiences. I thank you that whether it is a scar, a limp, or memory those things are proof I have overcome something. I thank you that I can stand in that truth, and I thank you for changing my perspective. Finally, I can see that there is nothing about my life that can stop me from fulfilling your plans for it. Today, I rejoice because you are a God that places great things inside of broken people. Thank you that your love heals broken people like me. *Thank you for my limp! Thank you for my scars! Thank you that you still have a plan for my life even with my deformities. Amen.*

DAY 29
The Benediction

Today I bring my relationship to you. At one point I believed you said, "he was my husband." Considering I was having sex with him that could have been my flesh talking. At this point in our relationship, I no longer desire to beg for a person's attention or convince them they are loved by me. If they want to be alone, I will give them that time. I wash my hands from trying to make it work. Our insecurities appear to have caused more damage than either one of us would care to admit. I cannot continue to convince him I love him and vice versa. I am willing to accept that now. I do not have the energy. I am exhausted, and I am tired of crying over the matter.

Maybe our experience was an introduction to the love You have in store for me. Maybe I was so invested in making us work because I wanted him to be my first and only sex partner. Truth is I loved that man from my soul, and all I have wanted to do is love him. After our first conversation, I knew I wanted to marry him. Now I sit with the reality of that may not be what is planned for my life, and to that I say, "It is well." I can rest knowing I gave all I had to this relationship. I have no regrets. I have learned more about love, life, and myself in his care. I realized that I can be loved beyond a physical affliction. I learned there is someone interested in teaching me how to Chicago Step in the kitchen. I learned there is someone interested in building an empire with the person they love. I also learned that insecurities can damage the greatest of relationships. I discovered our unchecked past will always come to rob you of a promising future. I have learned that after the words are spoken, and before damage is done, walking away may be the safest thing to do. This is the one relationship that I can admit I gave a fighting chance, and I am proud of the fight we gave it. I simply bow out gracefully and leave it in God's hands. If it is truly for me, it will happen. I quit or better yet, I surrender to whatever God's will is for my life this season. I am done trying to manipulate things. I am finished trying to convince him of the love I have for him.

FREEDOM QUESTIONS:

1. Is there a relationship in your life that requires a benediction?

2. Does this relationship draw you closer to God or away from him? If you answered away from God, why are you clinging to something that is pulling you away from the Source of your life?

3. What is the real reason(s) that you have been holding on to it?

4. If you have been sexually active with the person, is the sex one of the reasons you are holding on to it?

5. Have you become so fixated on being married that you are willing to overlook the red flags in exchange for the white dress or black tuxedo?

6. Do you genuinely love the person, or do you love the fact you have a relationship?

7. Are you in love with who they are or who they have the potential to become? If you answered the potential of who they can become, would you be able to love them as they are if they never became who you wanted them to become?

FREEDOM ASSIGNMENT:

Consider the person you are currently dating. Do not consider their potential or the dreams you two have shared. Consider them as they currently are: their habits, ideologies, health, education, etc. Based on the knowledge you currently have about them, write out what the next 3-5 years of your life would look like with them as they are today. Then ask yourself is this someone I want to marry. If the answer is "no," let the relationship go so that they can find someone who wants them. If the answer is "yes," but the person has shown by their actions they do not desire to commit to you, let it go! You deserve to be with someone who wants you.

FREEDOM PRAYER:

God I am so tired of chasing people in hopes of being loved by them. I am tired of giving my heart to people who are incapable of protecting it. I am tired of allowing the desire for marriage to rush me into relationships. I repent for engaging in fornication and putting my desire for love above your call to righteousness. Today I ask that you give me the strength to end any relationship that keeps me from you. I repent for making men my Lord. Today, I make you the Lord of my life and lover of my soul again. Amen

DAY 30
A Bleeding Heart and an Anguished Soul

I will be glad and rejoice in your unfailing love for you have seen my troubles, and you care about the anguish of my soul. You have not handed me over to my enemies, but you have set me in a safe place. Psalm 31:7,8

I find it interesting that you can break up with a man in hopes of it bringing you peace, and you still find yourself stressed out over how to handle life after it. I have almost driven myself mad trying to figure out what is next; and whether I have missed my opportunity to FINALLY be a man's wife. As anxiety attempted to ruin my morning, I felt a prompting to turn my bible to Psalm 31:6. I immediately start weeping at this beautiful reminder that God knows the condition of my heart. It is with this assurance that I am going to surrender it all to God. I am going to trust that there is no good thing that He would uphold from those who walk upright." I am going to focus on fulfilling my purpose and fixing the things I have neglected in my personal life.

I have been under this illusion that my wholeness would come from being connected to someone else. However, I have discovered that two people will destroy each other trying to love one another with broken hearts. I have some emotional baggage and physical things that need my undivided attention.

I am quite certain that if I do not deal with these things this time, I am going to be in the same situation with someone else. I manage to fall in love with severely emotionally damaged men in hopes that my love would restore them. However, without fail, I get hurt because hurt people truly do hurt people. This Savior mentality has caused me great pain, and now I am the emotionally damaged one. If I do not deal with the brokenness in my heart, I too will become a hurt person that hurts people. In my efforts to find love and be loved, I have become a casualty of war. Now I am in the infirmary with a bleeding heart that only the Chief Heart Surgeon can heal. God please heal this heart of mine.

FREEDOM QUESTIONS:

1. What has been the most difficult part about your breakup?

2. If you were in a "situationship," what was the most difficult part about getting over someone that did not want a relationship with you?

3. What wounds are you carrying from past relationships that you are expecting a new relationship to heal in you?

4. When are you going to stop making others responsible for fixing the things you know are broken inside of you?

5. When was the last time that you spent time learning

to love yourself instead of trying to convince others to do it for you? If your answer is "never," when do you plan on doing it?

6. What were your dreams and goals before you started dreaming or living life with your significant other?

7. Have you achieved any of those things yet?

8. What areas of your life have you neglected?

9. What are the things that you have said you wanted to do with your future spouse? List them.

10. Consider the list you just created, if you are never married, how much of your life did you put on hold waiting from them to show up?

FREEDOM ASSIGNMENT:

For the next 3-6 months, GET BACK TO YOU! Go back to the list of goals and dreams you had for yourself and start working towards them. Do not date anyone except yourself. In other words, GO OUT and enjoy your own company.

FREEDOM PRAYER:

God, I surrender my damaged heart. I acknowledge that I have gone on countless pursuits of finding love, affirmation, and acceptance. I repent for trying to find love outside of you. You should have been my pursuit this entire time. I have given so much of me to other people. It is time that I put more of an effort into strengthening my relationship with you. I am tired of seeking love from broken people who are incapable of filling the voids inside of me. Thank you for every experience that has brought me to this place. Thank you for the grace to keep this vow, and my only desire from this pursuit is to know you and be healed by your unfailing love. Amen

DAY 31
The Wound that Never Heals

Today something happened that was bittersweet. My father's son reached out to me. After telling me a few years ago, I was misinformed about being my father's daughter. I did not feel like trying to convince him, so I just left it alone. This morning I received an Inbox Message apologizing and asking if he could come meet my sister and I. He left his number asking, "Would I call?" I did. The conversation was a sweet one. He was very apologetic, and he shared his side of the story. I soon found out my father denied us to him and his mother. He told them we were not his, and two hours after our conversation I am sitting here sobbing at the fact a man who loved my mom denied us as his children to his children. He claimed everyone but us, and now I do not know how to feel because I just thought he did not want to be around. I did not know he was telling people we were not his and making my mom out to be some crazy woman.

This thing seems to be the never healing wound of my life. Each time I try to be the bigger person and forgive, stuff keeps coming up!!! I know the bible says 70 times 70, but I am so sick of hurting behind someone else decision to leave, lie, and neglect his responsibility. It is hard growing up as a kid with the gift of discernment. Being able to feel people playing nice but knowing something was off about the situation.

This has brought back so many things I have tried to discard from my memory. Like never feeling good enough to be an Evans and too light to be a real Porter. I remember the cold shoulders my dad's brothers would give my sister and I when they saw us. Never saying anything to my mom about it, but knowing we were not quite welcome. It is a real strange feeling as a kid to pick up an adult's disdain towards you, and you did nothing to merit it. It was almost this unspoken rule of the Evans family that if you did not come from marriage you did not exist, or that was my experience with my father's brothers. My aunts have always been sweet, warm, and welcoming. But at this moment, I find myself pissed, and I have no desire to be an Evans.

This is more overwhelming than I care to admit. My heart is in excruciating pain. It was one thing to wrestle with abandonment; but finding out your father was denying you is a completely different pain. It used to be the five years old in me that needed healing from abandonment. Now, it is the almost 31 years old woman that needs to be healed from rejection. God I am unable to heal myself. I leave my pain at your feet. I give it all to you, and I receive your love for me. I choose to forgive every person that has hurt me in this situation, and I refuse to be bitter behind what was shared today. It was the past, and that is where I leave it in Jesus name Amen!

FREEDOM QUESTIONS:

1. What is the issue(s) in your life that always has a way of producing pain when it resurfaces?

2. Why is it so difficult to make peace with the person or place that is responsible for that pain?

3. Does the issue find a way to find you, or are you always relieving it for pity purposes?

4. How would forgiving all parties involved change your life?

5. What is stopping you from forgiving them today?

FREEDOM PRAYER:

God I am tired of reliving the pain of this experience. I am tired of the never-ending saga it has been in my life. Today I give it to you. I choose to forgive every person involved. I choose to no longer allow it to control my life. I give every feeling of rejection, resentment, anger, bitterness, and abandonment to you. May I find joy and peace in knowing your love for me. Amen.

DAY 32
One Prayer Didn't Fix It!

I assumed writing in my journal and saying that prayer had solved my heartache; but I woke up this morning and I was still sad. Even now as I write tears flow. Yesterday was the first time in my life that I heard my father went around denying my sister and I. He told my brothers to their face we were not his! Who does that? I mean it was one thing to stop being active in our lives, but it is a completely different thing to deny us to our other siblings. This man did not only disrespect us, but he disrespected my mom, a woman who still spoke highly of him after his departure. This will take some more prayer, and each time I am reminded of it I will choose to forgive until the sting has left. This year of my life has been the strangest and most painful of all. I have lost so much, but I have been finding myself in the process. This hurts like hell, but I am looking to Heaven to heal the sorrow my time on earth has created.

Hurting but Hopeful,
Charity Israel

FREEDOM QUESTIONS:

1. Describe your family life.

2. Is there anyone that you have a hard time forgiving because of their actions towards you? If so, list their name.

3. What things have they done or said that makes it difficult to forgive them? Write them out.

4. When the thought of their treatment towards you come to mind, do you throw yourself a Pity party or offer up a prayer to God?

5. When are you going to trust God with the pain they have caused your heart?

FREEDOM ASSIGNMENT:

Using the list from question 2, write a letter to each person stating the offense(s) you are holding against them. Close each letter with "I FORGIVE YOU!" If you need to give the letter to those individuals, I encourage you to do it. Do whatever it takes to free your heart and mind from their control.

FREEDOM PRAYER:

God thank you for the power to truly forgive those who have hurt me. Today, heal my heart from the wounds caused by my family. Bring all the pain to the surface so that it can be removed for good this time. I am tired of walking around with anger, resentment, bitterness, sorrow, and hate in my heart. Today I stop trying to fix me, and I surrender to your power to heal the brokenhearted. Thank you for healing my heart. Amen!

DAY 33
A Gift to my Dad

"Honor your father and mother. Then you will live a long, full life in the land the Lord your God is giving you." Exodus 20:12 New Living Translation

Today is Father's Day, and that has always been a holiday I wish could go away. It is the one holiday I cannot celebrate as I desire. I would love to lavish my dad with gifts and high praises, but his absence has prevented me from doing so. With the events that have transpired in the last few days, I have questioned whether I want him back in my life. Nevertheless, he is my father, and I must honor him for that reason alone.

Last year after my grandmother's funeral we embraced for the first time in 25 years. He apologized, and I quickly offered him forgiveness. I attempted to cultivate our relationship, but I was the one putting forth the effort. So, I decided to let things be as they have always been. I decided I would just continue to live my life as I had for the last 25 years, without him. I had grown accustomed to it. I already had my first date. I already learned how to ride a bike, and I was an adult that has managed to do pretty good for herself despite his absence.

As I pulled myself out of the pit of sadness I was in, I had to face a reality about me and my dad's relationship. During his absence, I had created the perfect father in my head. Every time something would occur, I would say to myself, "If my father was here it would have gone this way." He was my hero in every situation that I felt his presence was needed. I would watch television and see men like Dr. Huxtable, Carl Winslow, and Phillip Banks and give my dad all their greatest characteristics. Although my imaginary dad was a coping mechanism for me, it created unrealistic expectations and disallowed my father to be himself in our relationship. The truth is my dad is different. His background did not produce a Phillip Banks. His background produced a broken man that has difficulty cultivating relationships with his children because his father did not cultivate one with him. His dad was a provider, but that was it. He became the man he resented, and his children suffered the same pain he did. Yes, he could have opted to be different; but doing the opposite of what has been done to you requires a different kind of strength that most are too afraid to use.

Knowing what I know about my father, I have three options: stay away from him.; keep my unrealistic expectations and keep getting hurt; or love him without conditions and give him the freedom to be who he is. I am going to choose Option 3 because that is how I desire people to be in relationship with me. I am letting go of what I expected a father to be and I will just allow him to be who he is.

We all deserve a chance to be ourselves and not be held by unexpressed expectations and preconceived notions of how our relationship will go. My dad will never be Carl Winslow or Dr. Huxtable, but I can give him the freedom to be himself. My Father's Day gift to him will be an apology and the gift of freedom from my expectations. He may be a little more complexed than I imagine; but he is mine and I must love him as he is or not at all...The road to restoration is a difficult one, but it's possible if both parties are interested in having it.

Staying Hopeful,
Charity Israel

FREEDOM QUESTIONS:

1. Describe your parents and the relationship you have with them.

2. List the expectations that you have for both of your parents.

3. Have they met, failed, or exceeded your expectations throughout the years? If you feel that your parent(s) failed you, complete this sentence: My parent failed me by _____.

4. Do you believe their failure is worthy of your forgiveness? Why or why not?

5. Considering what you know about your parents, have your unspoken expectations interfered with the relationship you have with them?

6. Considering what you know about your parents, are your expectations the cause of the constant disappointment you experience with him or her?

7. In the reading I said, "knowing what I know about my father, I have three options: stay away from him; keep my unrealistic expectations and keep getting hurt; or love him without conditions and give him the freedom to be who he is." Have you accepted your parents for who they are or are you still trying to make them fit the mold you created for them?

8. What would your relationship with your parents looked like if you gave them the freedom to be themselves? (If freedom to be themselves causes you physical or mental anguish, it is fine to stay away from them).

9. When will you release your parents from your expectations? How about today?

FREEDOM PRAYER:

Today, I choose to forgive my parent(s) for all the things they failed to do. I repent for holding an offense against them because they did not meet my expectations. Help me to accept my parents and love them with no strings attached. You have been so kind to love me as I am, help me to extend that same kindness to my parents. Amen.

DAY 34
Confronting Jealousy

I am embarrassed to admit it, but I must tell the truth. This season of my life requires I confront what pains me; acknowledge what I did wrong; and move pass it. So here goes... Something amazing happened in my sister's life as it pertains to Social Media exposure. Within the last couple of days, she has gone from roughly 750 fans to 30,000 or so. As someone who knows the struggle she has faced trying to accept her gift of laughter, I am in awe and rejoice. However, those evil twins, jealousy and envy, have popped their heads up out of my heart.

As someone who has been giving energy to building my audience for years, and just reaching close to 4,000 on Facebook, the jealousy in me was evoked. Wondering once again, why does she get all the great opportunities? She does not seem to chase after God as I do. However, all the good stuff always happen in her life, while I am forced to be in the background. It hurts to even admit that I am envious of my sister considering how much I love her. She is and has been my best friend. I love the fact that her hard work is paying off, and I know it is God's doing.

Jealousy and envy does not care about what relationship it attacks, and the reason for the feelings are often irrational. If I cannot handle her social media success, how am I going to handle the real-life success that we have been praying for since children? Truth is I am not owed anything by anyone in this world. If I cannot rejoice for the person who has been there for me more than anyone else on this planet, I have some real issues. Truth is I am grateful for this moment revealing my heart. I love my sister to life, and I want to be with her every step of the way cheering for her success from a pure place without ulterior motives.

God, I repent for being jealous and envious of my sister's success. Lord I ask that you continue to grant her success and favor. I love my sister, and I will not allow jealousy or envy to ruin our relationship. God work out of my heart anything that would sabotage the relationships of those I love the most. It would be tragic not to genuinely support those you claim to love. I do not ever want to know that kind of hypocrisy; and thank you for shining the Truth of your love in that area of my life. Remove jealousy and envy far from my heart and replace it with a love that supports, celebrates, and is genuinely happy for everyone in my life. If there is anyone else I have found myself jealous or envious of throughout the years, I repent. I repent for every moment I thought I was entitled to something of someone else. I repent for every time I felt someone owed me because of what I did for them in their time of despair. I repent for every time I pretended to celebrate with someone when I was in fact envious and or jealous of what they acquired. Lord I repent for believing that the good I do, and the time I spend in your presence makes me privy to any and every earthly possession. The covenant I have with you is spiritual, and the prosperity of my soul is your main concern. Keep me mindful that if it is not from a genuine place do not do it in hopes of what you may get out of it. Thanks again for exposing the darkness of my heart and as I have confessed and repented, I thank you that I am free to love not just my sister but everyone from a pure heart.

FREEDOM QUESTIONS:

1. Have you ever struggled with being jealous or envious of a person?

2. What were some of the reasons you felt this way towards them?

3. While reading this entry, did anyone come to mind that you love but find yourself jealous or envious of?

4. If yes, have you been honest about your feelings towards them or have you tried to convince yourself that you could not be jealous or envious?

FREEDOM ASSIGNMENT:

Get in a quiet place and confess your true feelings about that person to God. Admit that you have been jealous and/or envious of their success, relationship, social status, etc. If you know your emotions have caused a rift in the relationship, humble yourself and ask for forgiveness from the person. Remember that there is no condemnation in Christ Jesus, once you have confessed it before God you should no longer be ashamed of your feelings or actions. Today you have an opportunity to be cleansed of the jealousy and envy that has polluted your heart. Ask God to remove those things from your heart and believe in faith that He has heard your request.

FREEDOM PRAYER:

Holy Spirit remove jealousy and envy far from my heart and replace it with a love that supports, celebrates, and is genuinely happy for everyone in my life. If there is anyone else I have found myself jealous or envious of throughout the years, I repent. I repent for every moment I thought I was entitled to something of someone else. I repent for every time I felt someone owed me because of what I did for them in their time of despair. I repent for every time I pretended to celebrate with someone when I was in fact envious and or jealous of what they acquired. Lord I repent for believing that the good I do and the time I spend in your presence makes me privy to any and every earthly possession. The covenant I have with you is spiritual, and the prosperity of my soul is your main concern. Thanks again for exposing the darkness of my heart and as I have confessed and repented, I thank you that I am free to love everyone from a pure heart. Amen

DAY 35
No Wedding, No Love: Life After Heartbreak

Wednesday night, I cried myself to sleep. Out of nowhere, it hit me that my dreams of marriage had been shattered once again. I started replaying the moments of excitement looking at rings, searching for a venue, and trying on dresses. I started to think about how I finally had someone who loved me and wanted me as his wife. This marriage was meant to be the validation I needed to prove that I am desirable. The abrupt departure of my father at age five had left me wondering will I ever be wanted and loved. I had come to see marriage as a form of redeeming that piece of me. On December 31, 2016 we had the breakup of all breakups, and my dream was shattered. All my hopes for us were robbed and " hope deferred makes the heart sick..." became my reality. (Proverbs 13:12)

I believe one of the greatest pains of our human experience is a broken heart. Its pain is piercing and relentless. With all the strength you possess you try quickly to move pass it, but broken things often heal slowly. You are simply forced to endure its pain. Some try to sedate it with sex, liquor, and drugs, but it refuses to leave. Some try to work it away, but the moment you take a break, it's there. Some try to reason it away, but heartache supersedes knowledge; and you will never truly understand why your heart hurts so bad.

One of my greatest fears was to be where I am now, and that's on the back side of a failed engagement. I read stories and met women who had gone through it; but I never wanted to be acquainted with its grief. Now three months removed from it today, I can testify there is life after it. The first 30 days consisted of bitter tears. I wept because I felt like I had wasted my time. I mourned because I loved him. I sobbed because I made the decision to call the relationship off. I lamented the death of the relationship because I had never been completely committed to a relationship the way I was with him (mind, body, and soul). I cried because I no longer saw myself part of his dreams.

I would be lying if I said this experience did not rip the fabric of the way I viewed love. It was almost successful in making me give up on it. I was almost convinced to never love again; but shutting myself off to loving someone keeps me from fulfilling my purpose. We were created to love. Choosing not to do so makes you defective as a person because you are not fulfilling the Great Manufacturer's purpose for creating you.

During the first 30 days, all I could remember was the broken promises. I had forgotten about all the joy and life our love had given me. Although the flaws of our humanity brought on the demise of our relationship, the love we shared was pure, healing, and refreshing. I learned so much about me, and I appreciate every lesson his love taught me. I assumed we were destined for forever, but it appears we were just made for a moment together. I truly am grateful for the time we shared together.

I am not sure what the future holds for me, and I am quite alright with its uncertainty. I no longer see marriage as the validation I needed to prove I am worthy of love. I rest in the fact that I was created to love, and at the appointed time that love will be received and reciprocated by the man it was created to serve. I am no longer bitter about the outcome, and I am hopeful that I will love again.

FREEDOM QUESTIONS:

1. Have you forgiven those who have hurt you in a romantic relationship? If not, list the names of the people who hurt you.

2. My heartbreak was due to a wedding that did not happen. What was the reason behind the pain you experienced?

3. How has that experience changed your perspective on life in that area?

4. Has your experience caused bitterness to reside in your heart?

5. Did any good come out of that painful moment, situation, or relationship?

6. Could focusing on what you gained renew your hope in a better future?

7. Matthew 6: 14 says, "For if you forgive other people when they sin against you, your heavenly Father will also forgive you." When are you going to forgive others as God has so graciously forgiven you?

FREEDOM PRAYER:

Dear God, here are the mangled pieces of my heart. I have been pretending that my heart is not in pain, but it needs your attention. I have allowed my experiences with others to turn me bitter, unforgiving, and cold. The situation invades my thoughts, and it interrupts my moments of joy. Today, I yield my pain to you. I forgive every person that has caused my heart harm in Jesus name. Amen.

DAY 36
What Kind of Mate are You?

There comes a point in life when you must choose to either confess or suppress the truth about yourself. You must look at your present situation and ask the frightening question, "How did I get here?" You must do some self-reflecting and be brutally honest about the role you played in your current state. After taking a journey within, here are a few truths I discovered about me and my behavior in relationships:

1. I have become a manipulator. There were moments when I manipulated things to get what I wanted. I could study a man and become whoever he wanted me to be. It's a cool thing to do until you have morphed so many times that you end up losing your real identity.

2. I have become a liar. I have told many white lies. I have exaggerated stories or stretched the truth on things that did not matter in hopes of obtaining their approval. You

cannot be a manipulator without being a liar. Even if it's a white one, it's still a lie.

3. I have become jealous. Due to previous relationships and their outcomes, I have found myself very jealous. I was a virgin until the age of 29, so majority of my relationships ended due to cheating. It became extremely difficult to trust men because cheating was something I started to expect from them. When I am single I do not have jealousy issues with women, but once I get involved with a man that ugly joker shows up EVERY SINGLE TIME!

4. I have become extremely insecure. Their cheating began to make me feel like I was not enough. It should be noted that every man that cheated said, "I cheated because I wanted to respect your virginity." I do not regret not sleeping with any of them, but their choice to cheat still caused me great pain. Each time was a shot to my self-esteem, and every woman became a threat to me.

5. I desire to be a wife. I would love nothing more than to be a good man's wife. I believe there is someone on this planet who could use what God has put inside of me. I believe there is a man who desires to build an empire with me as his wife. I truly desire someone I can spend the rest of my life with helping make this world a better place and enlarging the kingdom of God together.

6. I do not believe I will get married. The history of my family suggests that Porter women either do not get

married or marry horrible men. It has been two failed prospects for me. They all get ghost before it's time to commit to marriage. That kind of hurt does something to your psyche, and you would rather just choose to be single than experience disappointment again.

God this is the truth about me concerning relationships. Five out of the six things I stated, do not reflect you. Manipulation, jealousy, a lying tongue, insecurities, and lack of faith all are traits of the enemy of my soul! I want to repent for operating in manipulation, living with jealousy, lying, being insecure, and not having faith. Remove far from me the things that will bring you shame in the way I conduct my relationships. I am tired of being hurt because of my past. I have confessed the truth about me. I thank you that I am forgiven. Thank you for a clean heart and a new perspective on love. Today ends the wicked ways that I have handled relationships. Thank you for completing this thing in me. Amen.

FREEDOM QUESTIONS:

1. What is your relationship status?

2. Are you happy with your current relationship status? Why or why not?

3. Take a moment to reflect on your romantic relationships. Do you make a habit of manipulating things for your benefit?

4. Have you ever lied to maintain the relationship or impress

your significant other?

5. Would you consider yourself to be a jealous person? If yes, what impact has your jealousy had on your relationships?

6. Jealous people are often insecure people. How does your insecurities sabotage the health of your relationship?

7. Has your current mate given you reason to be insecure, or are you making them pay for things from your past relationships?

8. When are you going to stop making your mate responsible for fixing your insecurities?

9. I talked about my family's history with marriage. Do you think you will be married? Why or why not?

FREEDOM ASSIGNMENT:

Take the next five minutes and write down the truth about who you are as a mate. Write down the things you hate to admit, but you know are true. Feel free to confess that you are selfish, insecure, narcissistic, etc. You have nothing to be ashamed of because you will be the only person reading it. The list you make will become prayer points for you until you see a change in your behavior. If your traits are causing physical, emotional, or verbal harm to someone please schedule an appointment with a therapist. A better version of yourself is within you, but it may require some professional help to access it. Please go see a counselor.

FREEDOM PRAYER:

God, I must confess that I have not been the greatest representation of you within my relationships. This is the truth about who I am (read off your list). Please forgive me for my terrible behavior towards those I claim to love. I was hurt, and I hurt others trying to protect myself from getting hurt again. Today, I give you this area of my heart. Please heal it. I am tired of it causing me pain and bringing harm to others. As it pertains to my future mate, I leave the mystery of it in your hands. I am fully convinced that anything that is necessary for my life's journey, you will provide it. Amen.

DAY 37
Church Folks

Church hurts can range from something minor as Sister Johnson refusing to speak every Sunday to something major like being sexually abused by a church member. Some of us have had our secrets told as "Prayer Gossip." Prayer gossip is when information is spread as a prayer request with no intentions of praying. For example, "Girl, pray for Sister Keisha. You know her husband has cheated on her again for the fourth time. He has not been home in weeks." Once "the request" is shared prayer is replaced by a discussion about Sister Keisha's relationship. Some of us have fallen prey to "The Preaching Casanova," who swept us off our feet. He or she sold us dreams of marriage and ministry and dumped us shortly after they received what they wanted. To add insult to injury, they marry someone shortly after being involved with you.

As long as we live in a sin-sick world, OFFENSES WILL COME (Luke 17:1, NKJV)! They will hurt and try to make their residence in our heart. They will move their friends, bitterness and resentment, in with them making it difficult to deal with others (Hebrews 12:15). Regardless of the size of the offense, if it hurts, we should deal with it. Here are a few tips to keep your heart free from these intruders:

1. Acknowledge and deal with the offense. Oftentimes when we are offended we do one of two things. Either we will discuss our hurt with everyone except the person who has offended us, or we will try to convince ourselves we are too spiritual to be offended. Both are the wrong way to handle an offense. Matthew 18:15 tells us, "If another believer sins against you, go privately and point out the offense...." If we have not had a discussion with God or the person about the offense, we need to leave everyone else out of it. We make matters worse when we spread discord over unresolved offenses. Please be advised that as long as your sanctified spirit is wrapped in flesh, you are susceptible to being offended. There is no such thing as being too spiritual to be offended. The spiritual thing to do is address it and not pretend as if it does not exist.

2. Make an allowance for them. As a Christian, it our responsibility to set aside some extra love for those who will offend us. As children, we would receive an allowance for completing our chores at the end of the week. The Apostle Paul encourages us to give an allowance to those who will hurt us. Ephesians 4:2-3 says, "Always be humble and gentle. Be patient with each other, making allowance for each other's faults because of your love. Make every effort to keep yourselves united in the Spirit, binding

yourselves together with peace." As flawed human beings, we will have moments that we do things out of selfishness, ignorance, and carelessness. When this happens, we must extend the same grace to people that we desire to be given in our less than Holy moments of human interaction.

3. Forgive them. Colossians 3:13 says, "Make allowance for each other's faults, and forgive anyone who offends you. Remember, the Lord forgave you. So, you MUST forgive others." I would expound on this, but I believe the scripture is self-explanatory. As Christians, we no longer possess the right to be unwilling to forgive. If we have accepted God's forgiveness for our sins, we must extend forgiveness to others for their sins toward us.

4. Forgive and prosecute. I believe every sin and offense is forgivable. However, consequences are attached to them. In the cases of church hurts involving sexual abuse, stealing, and anything the laws of our land have set rules against, prosecution to the full extent of the law is the consequence for that offense. There are too many sexual predators and robbers posing as Christians hurting Christians. We can still extend the love of Christ to them via a prison cell. Please use wisdom! Do NOT take Sis. Williams to court over the five dollars she borrowed from you two years ago.

We have a choice to live in the freedom forgiveness offers or as prisoners to the offenses of our past. My hope is that we will evict bitterness, resentment, and the offenses from our hearts. We are no good to a hurting world if we are hurting. Let this day end with your heart free. If counseling is needed, please seek it. If you need to press charges, God will be your strength. Remember: OFFENSES WILL COME so set aside some extra love, grace, and forgiveness for those who will sin against you.

FREEDOM QUESTIONS:

1. Are you currently offended by someone in the church?

2. When someone offends you how do you usually handle it?

3. Do you handle your offenses differently from what Matthew 18: 15 instructs us to do as Christians?

4. Who are the people in your life that need forgiveness?

5. When are you going to make an allowance for them and forgive?

6. Is there anyone that has committed a crime against you that needs to be prosecuted? If so, please do what will bring you peace and protect others from the same crime.

FREEDOM PRAYER:

Father forgive me for not handling offenses properly. I have held grudges for far too long, and I have withheld forgiveness from those who hurt me. Today, I thank you for the grace to do things your way. I thank you for giving me the wisdom on both the tone and timing to address the offense. Thank you for the allowance you gave me through Jesus Christ. I will make more of an effort to make allowance for others. Amen.

DAY 38
Dear Daddy: A Letter to the man who Raised Me

Today marks the one-year anniversary of your passing (September 3, 2012), and I must admit I have not been able to write about this for a year. But I suppose doing so will put my mind at ease and thoughts of our past to rest. I first want to say "THANK YOU" for rearing two girls that were not your own. It is no secret that we did not have the best of relationships due to some of your personal life decisions; but I must acknowledge the effort you put forth. After leaving home and having to face or suppress my own demons, I understand your internal conflict that we had to physically witness. I understood your need for escape and your temporary leave of absence from your responsibilities as a husband and a father. I understand why you chose certain things to help you cope with failure, unrealized dreams, and the desire to do better but not quite "getting it together."

I appreciate you staying away at your darkest times and returning when daybreak arrived. I appreciated your charisma. During your good days, you gave love and laughter to everyone around you. I am grateful for our verbal sparring. You taught me how to stand up for myself. I also apologize for them. I should have been more respectful.

We had this talk before but know that I FORGIVE EVERYTHING said that took a blow at my confidence, my talents, and my dreams. I now know your greatest pain in life was coping with your unrealized dream. Until the day of your funeral, I did not know you made history and set Basketball records in high school and college that have yet to be broken. I did not know I was living with an Urban Legend until your friends shared stories of the Glory Days with us. I am sorry I never took the time to get to know you.

Cole would be around, but you got to see God before I did. You were always good for surprises. I know you are safe now and free from a world that was not so kind to you. You were a troubled man, but I am grateful your last days were full of the rest you needed. You will be missed and thought of at every event. Maybe we can dance together when I get to heaven since you won't make my wedding. What I know about a good but severely broken man I learned from you, and no matter the dysfunction that plagued my childhood I will only hold on to the good.

Thanks for Trying,
Your Eldest Daughter

FREEDOM QUESTIONS:

1. Was there an adult from your childhood that gave you a hard time growing up? If so, what is their name?

2. Describe the relationship and how it affects you now as an adult.

3. Did the use of drugs and alcohol play a role in the way that person treated you?

4. Are you at peace with your past experiences with them, or is the wound just as fresh as the day it happened?

5. How does holding on to those memories help your mental, emotional, and physical health?

6. Considering what you know about that individual(s) past, are you able to move pass what they did for the sake of your own freedom? Why or why not?

FREEDOM ASSIGNMENT:

Letters are often therapeutic because they give you an opportunity to express your thoughts without being interrupted. Write a letter to the person that made your childhood a traumatic experience. Tell the person who caused you the most pain growing up what they did to you; and how their actions caused you to live with certain insecurities, fears, and torment. Once you have expressed the pain, tell them of your strength, resilience, and their inability to destroy you as they intended. Finish the letter with "I forgive you." Write as many letters as you need to write. Whether the person is dead or alive, free your heart from the pain they caused you. You may discover that you need some assistance dealing with your pain. Please allow a counselor the opportunity to assist you in becoming whole in that area of your life.

FREEDOM PRAYER:

God I thank you that your presence is a healing balm to my hurting soul. Each letter today was my Emancipation Proclamation from that pain and that season of my life. Today, I am set free from their words, the pain, and that season of my life. Today I can start fresh, and I'm grateful that you are the God that restores those who are damaged, broken, and hurting. Amen

DAY 39
Dear Love

It has been awhile since we have seen each other, and your presence is greatly missed. The first time we met, I was frightened by you. I questioned "why would you want me, and what made me worthy of you?" Out of fear, I abused you. Thinking I would be rejected, I neglected you. You had no choice but to leave. Please forgive me for pushing you away.

The second time you came around, I was determined to make it work. After experiencing the beauty of you, I wanted to prove I had learned to accept you. So I put up with a lot and ignored many signs because I did not want to let you down. I was so in need of the high you gave, I yielded my heart to someone who did not completely understand you. I suffered greatly trying to manufacture something as divine as you. In the process of desperately wanting to experience you, I paid a high price. I cashed in my self-respect, standards, dignity, and my faith (almost).

I wanted you so bad, but you were not present. Once this synthetic or faux love came to an end, my heart was completely hardened. I was remorseful that I tried to force your return. I was bitter because I knew it was not you; and I allowed the façade to go on too long. I was hurt. Trying to create Love is far more painful than waiting on you. I owe you an apology for imitating you and becoming so bitter that I started to question your existence. The next time I am blessed with your presence, I will receive you with open arms. I will not question why you returned. I will not question whether I am worthy of you. I know that I am.

When I am certain it is you, I will gladly give you my heart. You can be trusted. There is no desire to reject you because you accept me. There is no need to impress you because you are completely into me. I now know I can trust you with my insecurities. I know you will not find the scars of my life repulsive. I am certain I can trust you with my fears because in your perfection, you take them away. I am convinced my past sins will not intimidate you because you cover a multitude of them.

I no longer fear you, and I will not rush your return. I will continue to prepare my heart for your residency. I am daily cleaning out my skeletons and facing my demons because You deserve my whole heart. It is open to you again. Know that I am preparing myself to receive and keep you next time. There will be no games you will have to win or walls you will have to break down. I no longer possess a list of how tall you are; how much you make; and what you must look like. I just want you in the package you choose to come in. You graciously accepted me, and I will extend that grace back to you.

Sincerely,
Your Beloved

FREEDOM QUESTIONS:

1. What is your definition of Love?

2. Have you ever been in love? Describe the experience.

3. Has there ever been a time that you rejected love from someone because you felt unworthy of it?

4. Who or what told you that you were unworthy of love?

5. Have you ever tried to make a person love you? How did that situation work out for you?

6. How did that situation change your perspective on love and relationships?

7. Could your perspective on love be the reason why Love has been distant from you?

8. Are you open to love again? Why or why not?

FREEDOM ASSIGNMENT:

I Corinthians 13: 4-7 describes Love as followed:

Love is patient and kind. Love is not jealous or boastful or proud [5]or rude. It does not demand its own way. It is not irritable, and it keeps no record of being wronged. [6]It does not rejoice about injustice but rejoices whenever the truth wins out. [7]Love never gives up, never loses faith, is always hopeful, and endures through every circumstance.

From this day forward, allow God's word to be your standard for understanding Love. With every relationship you enter, romantic or platonic, allow this to help you determine if the Love is real. Also it should hold you accountable for how you treat others. If you have discovered that your love does not look like I Corinthians 13:4-7 description, ask the Holy Spirit to teach you how to love. If you discover the "love" you are currently experiencing does not fit that description, ask for wisdom on how to fix it or leave that relationship.

FREEDOM PRAYER:

God, thank you so much for your love. Today, I give you my heart, and I ask that you make me receptive to love again. I place every relationship and encounter with people that has tainted my perception of it at your feet. I repent for causing pain to anyone, including myself, due to my misunderstanding of it. I thank you that I Corinthians 13:4-7 can now be the standard by which I give, receive, and understand Love. I look forward to experiencing it as you intended in Jesus name. Amen!

DAY 40
Let Freedom Ring

"Lord, you will grant us peace; all we have accomplished is really from you. ^{13}O Lord our God, others have ruled us, but you alone are the one we worship. ^{14}Those we served before are dead and gone. Their departed spirits will never return! You attacked them and destroyed them, and they are long forgotten. ^{15}O Lord, you have made our nation great; yes, you have made us great. You have extended our borders, and we give you the glory!"-Isaiah 26:12-15

Today is the last day, and this scripture came to my heart as I was preparing for devotions. Considering all the things I have confronted in the last 39 days, this feels like a confirmation that this journey has not been in vain. I have been guilty of worshipping many idols, but the time I have spent in your presence has crushed them. Many things have been Lord of my life, but this time together ended their reign. I have desperately longed to live as a new creation, and I am now confident that I can because of Jesus Christ. 2 Corinthians 5:21 says, "For God made Christ, who never sinned, to be the offering for our sin, so that we could be made right with God through Christ." When Jesus became the offering for my sins, he took the power of those sins over my life to the cross. They are no longer rulers and lords of my life. Christ's resurrection sealed the deal. His authority over death and the grave makes my new life possible (Revelation 1:18).

I am now empty of the shame that gripped my life for the last 30+ years. I am no longer ruled by fear, but I am powered by love and faith. I have confessed everything! Nothing about me is hidden from God, and I am no longer ashamed of me. As painful as it was to lose everything, I am eternally grateful that it happened! All those things kept me distracted from living the life God had planned for me. They created a false sense of security, love, accomplishment, and success. I now see the miracle in what appeared to be madness in my life! I now believe God truly loves me.

Everything that could ever hold me prisoner has been placed in Christ's hands (the power of sin, death, and the grave). I have nothing to fear or be ashamed of in this life. My freedom is in Christ alone, and my identity has been transformed because of him. 2 Corinthians 5:17 says, "That anyone who belongs to Christ has become a new person. The old life is gone; a new life begun." I have been a Christian for 24 years; but I am now coming to realize the beauty of being a new creation. Freedom is a beautiful thing, and I'm grateful my freedom has been found in Christ. Knowing I can now take full advantage of my new life in Christ has made the journey well worth it.

FREEDOM QUESTIONS:

Day 6 — God is teaching how to live

1. What are three things that you learned about God while reading this book? *He is in me. His Peace. His Forgiveness. He holds me close.*

2. How have those things changed your relationship with him? *I love God beyond words.*

3. What three things did you learn about yourself while reading this book? *Some past experiences are no longer issues.*
   * *I learned also that I need to speak up*
   * *I need to manifest and clarify what I want. (Define)*

4. Have you developed a greater love for yourself and your journey through reading this book? *Yes. I am working on accepting more people and letting people help me.*

5. What are three things that you learned about how you relate to others while reading this book?
   I am gentle, patient, respectful and honest. because I need that myself.

FREEDOM PRAYER:

God thank you for the growth that has occurred in the last 40 days. Thank you for the freedom that has come to my heart because of it. Today, I ask that you teach me how to remain free from the things I have confessed to you during this journey. I am now convinced that whom the son sets free is free indeed. Thank you for the freedom! Amen.

Congratulations on completing the book. To download your certificate of completion, please visit the link at: chairityisrael.net/certificate-of-completion/

Made in United States
Orlando, FL
25 January 2022

14004083R10095